MISGUIDED BADGES

MISGUIDED BADGES

A PERSONAL MEMOIR

THEN & NOW:

"Police Officers Who Continually Defy Public Trust, Abuse Authority and Deny the Truth."

"The Time Is Always Right to Do What Is Right"
-- *Martin Luther King, Jr.*

by
CAPTAIN D. TERRY YARBROUGH (Ret.)
Shelby County Sheriff's Office
Memphis, Tennessee

Misguided Badges

Book and Cover design by Pamela D. Cox

ISBN: 978-1-7377017-0-5 (Print)

ISBN: 978-1-7377017-1-2 (Digital)

First Edition

Printed in the United States of America.

Scriptures are taken from the KING JAMES VERSION (KJV): KING JAMES VERSION, public domain.

Psalm 121

*"I will lift up mine eyes unto the hills,
from whence cometh my help.
My help cometh from the Lord, which made
heaven and earth."*

Romans 8:31

*"What shall we then say to these things?
If God be for us, who can be against us?"*

"Truth, Trust, and Accountability do matter. Misguided police officers, *aka Misguided Badges,* must embrace 'the truth' about the American policing culture and systemic racism for the greater good of public trust, public integrity, and public perception. RACIAL BIGOTRY, IGNORANCE, and HYPOCRISY should never define our policing culture. Learning to understand other people is crucial for racial healing and establishing positive relationships. The American policing culture must conform to the Constitutional rights granted to every American citizen, regardless of race, ethnicity, gender, or skin color." *-- DTY*

Table of Contents

FOREWORD

On March 9, 2020, **Terri Stephanie Thornton,** my daughter, surprised her dad with a birthday gift packet labeled, *Start Writing Your Book Today.* She inspired me to end my procrastination with the writing of a Memoir. I was truly blessed.

As Americans, police officers and citizens shall obey the Rule of Law in pursuit of equal justice under the law, regardless of race, ethnicity, gender, or skin color.

The Memoir reflects the firsthand experiences, career challenges, and policing philosophy of a retired Black deputy sheriff captain born and raised in Memphis, Tennessee.

It exposes systemic racism, identifies a broken policing culture, reveals racial hypocrisy, offers constructive insight, and sheds light on a "Black Police Officer's Experience" lived in Memphis, Tennessee.

It suggests that essential police reforms are inevitable amid systemic racism continually tarnishing American democracy, dividing misguided police officers and Black citizens.

I am deeply grateful to the friends, citizens, and donors who nobly support law enforcement and community action partnerships for safer communities.

Ms. Kymyatta Fluellen, thanks for your help. The little things really do count.

Ms. Jeraldine Franklin-Sanderlin, I am forever grateful for your friendship, kindness, and support.

DEDICATION

MISGUIDED BADGES, a Memoir, reveals the boyhood experiences, career experiences, and policing philosophy of a retired Black police captain in Memphis, Tennessee. It exposes systemic racism, abusive practices, and discriminatory behavior perpetuated by Misguided Police Officers within a broken American policing culture.

I proudly dedicate this Memoir to three special people I had the pleasure of influencing as a father – **Michael, Terri Stephanie, and Sheree.** Nothing is more gratifying than bestowing honor to a son and two daughters. They often reminded me to author a book about the firsthand experiences that impacted my boyhood and life as a police officer. As children, they were fond of the quotes of wisdom I shared with them. For example: *"A winner never quits; A quitter never wins."*

I apologize for any inconveniences I caused with my parental persistence. I viewed my teachable moments as doing the right thing, passing along common-sense wisdom acquired from *"Granddaddy and Lil Mama."* Both thoroughly indoctrinated me with knowledge when I moved in with them at seven years of age. Moreover, I believe Michael, Terri Stephanie, and Sheree clearly understood my genuine concern for their future. They inspired me to provide a realistic learning resource for the next generation of the family.

Finally, I send a deserving shout-out to **my loving wife, Linda.** Thank you so much for your Faith, Patience, and Words of Encouragement.

The International Association of Chiefs of Police (IACP) Law Enforcement Code of Ethics, a universal model, provides ethical standards and guidelines for professional law enforcement officers.

However, the question looms, *"What is it that motivates Law Enforcement Officers to defy their oath of office, abuse authority, and deny the truth?"* Perhaps many of the answers or excuses by Misguided Police Officers will be far from good judgment. We must remember, "Law Enforcement Officers shall uphold the law; they are not above the law." -- DTY

LAW ENFORCEMENT CODE OF ETHICS

As a law enforcement officer, my fundamental duty is to serve the community; to safeguard lives and property; to protect the innocent against deception, the weak against oppression or intimidation, the peaceful against violence or disorder; and to respect the constitutional rights of all to liberty, equality, and justice.

I will keep my private life unsullied as an example to all and behave in a manner that does not bring discredit to me or my agency. I will maintain courageous calm in the face of danger, scorn, or ridicule; develop self-restraint, and be constantly mindful of the welfare of others. Honest in thought and deed, both in my personal and official life, I will be exemplary in obeying the law and the regulations of my department. Whatever I see or hear of a confidential nature or that is confided to me in my official capacity will be kept ever secret unless revelation is necessary for the performance of my duty.

I will never act officiously or permit personal feelings, prejudices, political beliefs, aspirations, animosities, or friendships to influence my decisions. With no compromise for crime and with relentless prosecution of criminals, I will enforce the law courteously and appropriately without fear or favor, malice, or ill will, never employing unnecessary force or violence, and never accepting gratuities.

I recognize the badge of my office as a symbol of public faith, and I accept it as a public trust to hold so long as I am true to the ethics of police service. I will never engage in acts of corruption or bribery, nor will I condone such actions by other police officers. I will cooperate with all legally authorized agencies and their representatives in the pursuit of justice.

I know that I alone am responsible for my standard of professional performance and will take every reasonable opportunity to enhance and improve my level of knowledge and competence. I will constantly strive to achieve these objectives and ideals, dedicating myself before God to my chosen profession, law enforcement. -- IACP

INTRODUCTION

The same racist attitudes, behavior, and practices manifested by Misguided Police Officers during the early days of slavery are prevalent today. Rational -- modern-day -- thinking should lead us to believe those days are far gone. Rampant incidents of police-involved shootings and alleged murders captured by video cameras show otherwise. Police departments must reconsider their hiring standards, training approaches, policy guidelines, and policing practices to satisfy 21st Century law enforcement precepts.

I avow that history is repeating itself right before our eyes. Dr. Martin Luther King, Jr. reminded us that "Silence is betrayal; speak out against this madness."

"Silence," reflected by *"Denial,"* is an indignity to the Law Enforcement Code of Ethics considering systemic racism, discriminatory practices, and police brutality. I fervently disavow the *"Blue Wall of Silence"* when exploited by misguided police officers to abuse authority, deny the truth, and defy public trust.

Civil Rights activists assert that Black citizens nationwide are disproportionately victimized by unreasonable, excessive force used by misguided police officers. I agree with this assertion as verified by indisputable video camera evidence of police-involved shootings and deaths across the country. Enough is enough. Excessive force must never be an acceptable policing practice to deliberately abuse any group of citizens. Policing practices that selectively and unjustly target Black citizens or people of color violate their constitutional rights and the core values of American democracy. Accordingly, I am persuaded that the American policing culture is broken; much healing is needed. I chose to speak out to raise awareness for building trust and bridging the divisive relationships between misguided police officers and Black citizens.

In the wake of high-profile, officer-involved shootings involving Black Americans, civilians, the media, and politicians have become increasingly critical of American policing. While new policies and technologies are aimed at addressing the public concern, there remains a lot of work to be done to improve the experiences of police officers and police culture (Miller & Ray, 2019).

MISGUIDED BADGES, a Memoir, discloses a philosophy of policing embraced during my 46-year law enforcement career. As intended, the Memoir is eye-opening, informative, and easy to read. The symbolic title represents *Misguided Police Officers* who – implicitly or explicitly -- demonstrate racial bias and resistance to equal justice under the law for all citizens.

My beliefs and opinions are based on firsthand experiences, news accounts, historical facts, and widespread police abuse. Changing the attitudes and behavior of *"Misguided Police Officers"* or *"Bad Apples"* can be a challenging task. Change may be uncomfortable when racial injustices and discriminatory practices are ingrained for so long. Pray that meaningful police reforms are forthcoming and callous attitudes will change. I remain prayerful and optimistic.

Speaking out truthfully might help warm cold hearts and change some narrow minds for the better. Who knows? It is certainly worth a try. Misguided police officers -- and biased politicians, too -- must face the truth and correct the obvious. Both are obstructive to advancing racial equality and equal justice for all citizens.

National news accounts and social media posts verify that White supremacy perspectives are openly endorsed by misguided police officers, right-wing politicians, and police organizations. I cherished this writing opportunity to illustrate how far Black people have come and must go. I am determined to speak out and encourage others -- Black, brown, and white – to rebuke systemic racism perpetuated to maintain *"White Privilege"* as superior in a diverse democracy.

I was born and raised in Memphis, Tennessee —South Memphis — where I saw White police officers create grief and spark outrage among Black citizens. Like Black neighborhoods in other cities, South Memphis faced police brutality and oppression for many years. Black neighborhoods were a source of pride and dignity for many of us. I am still defensive of my grassroots heritage with all heart and soul. Let it be understood; I make no excuses for the lawbreakers or criminals who deliberately committed crimes, including those who do so today.

As a little boy, I saw White patrol officers stop and abuse Black men and boys for no visible reason. It angered me to see and hear them call an elderly Black man a *"boy." "Hey, boy," "Come here, black ass Nigger,"* and *"Where you Niggers going"* were common insults we heard almost every day.

As a teenager, I experienced verbal abuse firsthand walking home late at night from a White restaurant job nearby. I often asked myself the question, *"Do cops have to treat Black folk this way?"* Strangely, this was one of the firsthand experiences that motivated me to become a Memphis police officer.

I felt there had to be a better way for White police officers to treat Black citizens. I grew up believing that all White officers were *"lowdown and dirty."* Their abusive behavior was the extent of what I saw. I finally dumped that ambiguous assumption after seeing White officers compassionately interact with Black citizens.

It is conceivable that most White police officers I witnessed abusing Black people became supervisors. They likely prevailed to pass along abusive behavior to others. Over the years, similar patterns of police abuse persisted -- as norms -- continually dividing police officers and Black citizens.

My motivation for writing Misguided Badges was not to cast aspersion on the Memphis Police Department or Shelby County Sheriff's Office. I applaud their national accreditation earned for commitment, excellence, and best practices. I wholeheartedly support their accredited mission to serve and protect the citizens of Memphis and Shelby County, Tennessee.

I will always praise and uplift the resolute men and women who serve honorably as police officers. Also, I embraced this writing opportunity to dispel any misguided notions that I am a racist or a radical with ulterior motives. The historical reality about the American policing culture and its link to systemic racism is an inescapable truth needing to be told for racial healing.

I speak from a Black man's perspective because I am Black. I intend not to degrade law enforcement, accuse, or demean any of my former partners and coworkers. I am grateful to survive and retire in good standing as a police officer and deputy sheriff. However, I must note that my on-the-job experiences and career challenges sharply contrasted those of my White partners or coworkers because of my skin color.

Frank Sonnenberg, a contemporary author and well-known advocate for moral character, personal values, and personal responsibility, once wrote, *"Always tell the truth, or the truth will tell on you."* I found Sonnenberg's moral quote the appropriate reminder for police officers, politicians, and citizens alike. I suggest that we take notice.

I refused to deny the truth and harbor a lie about the American policing culture. Unfortunately, acknowledging the truth about our policing culture was extremely uncomfortable for misguided police officers. Their stubborn *"Us vs. Them"* mindset continued to be hypocritical, corrupt, and unwilling to accept change.

Let the chips fall where they may. I witnessed that wrongdoing committed by misguided police officers often mirrors the racist attitudes and behavior of their supervisors. Racist police supervisors are likely to distort information to gain favor, enable or cover up misconduct committed by subordinates. Racist supervisors must be identified, held accountable, and corrected with certainty. They are part of the problem instead of a solution to correct the problem. Good supervisors set good examples, demand accountability, and communicate directly without compromising complaints or investigations.

Police officials must search their hearts and souls and come to grips with meaningful police reforms. Too many police supervisors, union representatives, and court prosecutors continually defend police officers who are *"Bad Apples."* Consequently, *"Bad Apples"* are emboldened to continue abusing authority, defying public trust, and denying the truth. As a Black police officer, I experienced racist attitudes and behavior, deliberate defiance, and denial of truth from *"Bad Apples"* and police officials throughout my career.

ONE

What Are Misguided Badges?

MISGUIDED BADGES, a Memoir, exposes police officers who violate their oath of office and the constitutional rights of others with racial disdain and disregard for laws, policies, rules, and regulations.

Misguided Badges symbolize police officers, *aka Bad Apples,* who perpetuate racial bias and maltreatment -- implicitly or explicitly -- while abusing their authority, defying public trust, or denying the truth.

Below are public news excerpts referring to police officers who could easily qualify as "Misguided Badges."

PROPUBLICA / January 14, 2021
"No One Took Us Seriously": Black Cops Warned About Racist Capitol Police Officers for Years by Joshua Kaplan and Joaquin Sapien *(This story is originally published by ProPublica)*

Allegations of racism against the Capitol Police are nothing new: Over 250 Black cops have sued the department since 2001. Some of those former officers now say it's no surprise white nationalists were able to storm the building (Kaplan & Sapien, 2021).

When Kim Dine took over as the new chief of the U.S. Capitol Police in 2012, he knew he had a severe problem. Since 2001, hundreds of Black officers had sued the department for racial discrimination. They alleged that white officers called Black colleagues slurs like the N-word and that one officer found a hangman's noose on his locker. White officers were called "huk lovers" or "FOGs" — short for "friends of gangsters" — if they were friendly with their Black colleagues. Black officers faced "unprovoked traffic stops" from fellow Capitol Police officers. One Black officer claimed he heard a colleague say, "Obama monkey, go back to Africa" (Kaplan & Sapien, 2021).

ASSOCIATED PRESS / June 6, 2019
Five States Investigates Racist, Violent Posts by Police

(AP) — Police departments in at least five states are investigating and, in some cases condemning, their officers' social media feeds after the weekend publication of a database that appears to catalog thousands of bigoted or violent posts by active-duty and former cops (Associated Press, 2019).

The posts were uncovered by a team of researchers who spent two years looking at police personal Facebook accounts from Arizona to Florida. They found officers bashing immigrants and Muslims, promoting racist stereotypes, identifying with right-wing militia groups, and, especially, glorifying police brutality. All the posts were public (Associated Press, 2019).

STAR NEWS ONLINE / June 24, 2020
'Wipe them off the map': Three Wilmington police officers fired for racist comments.

WILMINGTON — Three Wilmington Police Department officers have been fired after being caught on a police vehicle camera making racist comments about local Black citizens, fellow officers, and the department's newly appointed police chief. Chief Donny Williams, officially promoted to the department's top position just a day prior, said Wednesday. The video of the men's conversations included "disrespectful language, hate-filled speech, referring to Black people as the n-word" (Ingram, 2020).

THE ROOT NEWS / June 15, 2019
Report: Hundreds of Police Officers Belong to Racist Facebook Groups

Reveal, a news website site run by the nonprofit Center for Investigative Journalism recently completed a months-long investigation into police officers' involvement with extremism on Facebook. The social media giant allows its users to create closed groups that share pictures, posts, and information among members who must gain permission from other members or administrators to see and post content within the group (Harriot, 2019).

They acknowledged that tens of thousands of police officers on Facebook and thousands of Facebook groups with hateful ideologies would have been impossible to uncover *all* the cops who are aligned with online racism (Harriot, 2019).

No one person or organization can change misguided police officers' rebellious attitudes and behavior; they must do it themselves. I pray for their self-realization and understanding that all humans are created equal in the sight of GOD. The hearts and minds of misguided police officers must change for the good of American democracy and all citizens.

The following North Carolina news piece is an example of state legislative police reforms headed in the right direction. I believe most state legislatures will do the right thing and pass similar bipartisan police reform bills to safeguard against misguided police officers or *"Bad Apples."*

THE ASSOCIATED PRESS / **September 2, 2021**
Bipartisan North Carolina police reforms signed by Cooper by Gary D. Robertson

RALEIGH, N.C. (AP) — A bipartisan police reform package was signed into law Thursday by North Carolina Gov. Roy Cooper, emphasizing the success of enacting provisions from a task force he commissioned following George Floyd's murder over panel recommendations left out.

Backers of the legislation, which received near-unanimous approval from the General Assembly, say it will rid departments of derelict officers and give mental health assistance to others on the force. The provisions address law enforcement shortcomings during a national focus on racial inequity and the deaths of Black residents at the hands of police, such as Floyd last year in Minneapolis (Robertson, 2021).

THE CRIME REPORT / **March 2, 2021**
Stop Turning Your Head: Black Cops Speak Out Against 'Blanket of Racism' by Isidoro Rodriguez

Even as states and municipalities around the country rush to respond to calls for better training and greater accountability in response to police killings of African Americans like George Floyd and Breonna Taylor, African American cops warn that little will change unless their agencies confront the internalized racism that continues to distort American policing.

"There is a blanket of systemic racism in policing, and someone has to acknowledge that we do have a problem," said Lynda Williams, President of the National Organization of Black Law Enforcement Executives (NOBLE).

"We can't change the past, but we can understand the past. Even if it comes down to the very foundation of law enforcement being created for slave patrols."

Williams, a former deputy assistant director of the United States Secret Service, as well as a former deputy sheriff in Augusta, Ga., believes the burden of addressing the problem of racism in policing falls, first and foremost, on leadership.

However, willful ignorance by the leadership feeds a culture that can have dangerous consequences for communities around the country (Rodriguez, 2021).

The Crime Report (TCR) is a nonprofit multimedia information and networking resource based at John Jay College of Criminal Justice in New York. TCR is published daily online staffed by working journalists in New York, Washington, D.C., and Los Angeles. TCR provides comprehensive reporting, informed commentary, and analysis of criminal justice news and research in the United States and abroad. Since 2008, The Crime Report remains the primary non-partisan source for information about all aspects of criminal justice for thousands of scholars, practitioners, students, and journalists across the nation (The Crime Report, 2008).

TWO

Changemakers

I am honored to recognize the first duly elected Black Sheriff of Shelby County, Tennessee, seven Black Memphis police leaders, and nine Black Memphis police officers hired in 1948. Six of the seven Memphis police leaders became Director of Police Services. In contrast, one leader became the first Black Chief of Police.

On August 2, 2018, Sheriff Floyd Bonner, Jr., was elected the 47th Sheriff of Shelby County, Tennessee. Sheriff Bonner's election was a commemorative, history-making honor and change-making outcome for Memphis and Shelby County.

The Memphis Police changemakers remembered are Director James E. Ivy, 1988-1991; Director Melvin T. Burgess, Sr., 1992-1994; Chief Eddie B. Adair, 1992-1994; Director Walter J. Winfrey, 1994-1999; Director James H. Bolden, 2003-2004; Director Toney C. Armstrong, 2011-2016; and Director Michael W. Rallings, 2016-2021. I am grateful to these men for their leadership achievement in the city of Memphis.

On May 4, 2021, another change-making law enforcement milestone occurred in Memphis, Tennessee. Cerelyn "CJ"

Davis, a Black female, 35-year police veteran, was confirmed by the Memphis City Council as the first woman Chief of Police. Before Memphis, Chief Davis held the same position for five years in Durham, North Carolina. She moved to the city of Durham with 30 years of police experience from Atlanta, Georgia. Chief Davis is also a former President of the National Organization of Black Law Enforcement Executives (NOBLE).

Looking back, the following points to police brutality concerns when Black citizens became outraged in 1948. Black citizens' concerns gave rise to hiring Black police officers. Those citizens became outraged and requested that Mayor E.H. Crump hire Black officers to ease racial tension created by the White police officers. The mayor, referred to as *"Boss Crump"* by Black citizens, cooperated and approved the request (Goggans, 2014). **The historical hiring marked the beginning of the *"Black Police Officers' Experience"* in Memphis, Tennessee.**

In 1948, the Memphis Police Department (MPD) welcomed the first nine publicized Black officers. The historical occurrence appeared in a new documentary titled *True Blue – Memphis Lawmen of 1948* (Goggans, 2014).

They were assigned to foot patrol the historic Beale Street area. According to Andrew "Rome" Withers, son of famed **Civil Rights-era photographer Ernest Withers,** one of the first nine Black officers, their roll call was on Beale Street, separate from the White officers. Withers said, "They could not arrest white people at all; they could only detain them until a White officer came" (Goggans, 2014).

The hiring occurred "After several African Americans were severely beaten and shot by White police officers. Residents became outraged. A community meeting was held by Mayor E.H. Crump, who promised to provide the Black community with their parks and recreational facilities to ease police brutality concerns. However, one woman stood up and expressed that they would like Black police officers instead. Crump concurred, and African Americans were allowed to apply for the police force" (Goggans, 2014). Captain Jerry Williams was one of the pioneer Black police officers hired to hit the Beale Street walking beat patrol in 1949.

Captain Jerry Williams

Captain Jerry Williams, *Honoree*

Black History Month Celebration, 2/22/20, NHBC of Memphis

As of July 2020, Captain Jerry D. Williams, 92, one of the pioneer Black police officers hired in Memphis, was doing well. On February 22, 2020, we had the pleasure of interacting with Captain Williams at New Hope Baptist Church of Memphis, my church. **Pastor Robert J. Matthews,** the senior pastor, featured Captain Williams as the keynote speaker at a Black History Program honoring Black police officers. Pictured above, left to right, are Deputy Chief Edwin Henderson (MPD Ret.), Sheriff Floyd Bonner, Jr. (SCSO), Pastor Robert J. Matthews (NHBC), Captain Jerry Williams (MPD Ret.) seated, Director Michael Rallings (MPD Ret.), Deputy Chief Gerald Perry (MPD Ret.), and Captain D. Terry Yarbrough (SCSO Ret.).

Williams captivated the audience by sharing some trailblazing experiences as a Black police officer. It was interesting to compare the following news account about his experiences to -- Then and Now.

Patrolman Wendell Robinson & Patrolman Ernest Withers

Before Williams and the 12 other Black patrolmen hit Memphis's streets in 1949, the city had only allowed African Americans to join the force after yellow fever had killed thousands in 1878 and left the police force short-staffed. As a child, Williams never dreamed of or desired becoming an officer. At 16, he landed a lucrative position at the Illinois Central Railroad, where he assumed he would work until retirement (Capriel, 2014). But he said rampant abuse of Black citizens by the Memphis Police Department changed his mind. "I was constantly harassed by police when I would get off work," Williams said. "They would stop me and check my pockets for no reason but to give me a hard time. They did this to everyone, and we were tired of it" (Capriel, 2014).

However, police commissioner Joseph Boyle was no civil rights advocate, and equality was not something he granted. The Black officers were not allowed to change clothes at the central precinct, attend roll call, or even testify in court hearings. (They were allowed to carry firearms but had to purchase the guns themselves). Instead, they were installed under an informal "police your own" initiative, expected to walk the beat of Black neighborhoods and curb impropriety like gambling, profanity, and prostitution (Rosen, 2017).

The officers were also prohibited from arresting whites, only detaining them, which meant that the complaining party sometimes dismissed those responding to a call with rolled eyes. Residents believed the officers to be impotent, a reality often enforced by tenured White officers who openly mocked and insulted their Black counterparts (Rosen, 2017).

One of the patrolmen, Jerry Williams, remembered his frustrations during a 2011 town meeting where he was honored for his service. At the time, it didn't feel like such a privilege:

When we had to give a traffic ticket to a White person, the White man would—he wanted to make sure that we knew he was white. He would stick his head out of the car to make sure that we knew he was white. We would call in from the beat every hour. So, this commanding officer at that time called me in and told me, he said, *'Williams.'* I said, *'Yes, sir.'* *'Did you give so and so a ticket down there on Beale and Hernando?'* I said, *'Yes, sir, I did.'* He said, *'I want to tell you, you give another White person a ticket, you won't have this job anymore'* (Rosen, 2017).

Williams eventually made homicide detective, exhibiting a tenacity that ultimately exhausted the prejudiced officers on the force. **Wendell Robinson,** another of the original nine, received attention for helping to break up a con game. In 1965, he was promoted to lieutenant after scoring higher than anyone in the department on the exam. He retired in 1980 (Rosen, 2017).

A second "class" of Black officers was hired in 1951. Still, it wasn't until the United States sued the city in 1974 over discriminatory hiring policies that their law enforcement truly began to evolve beyond racial boundary lines. Today, half of the city's police force is made up of men and women of color. While it hasn't eliminated racial discord on the police force or in the town, the advancement toward that goal arguably began with the nine men who suited up in 1948—even if they had to do it outside the precinct (Rosen, 2017).

Like the first nine publicized Black police officers hired in Memphis, many of us have endured challenging sacrifices to have influence for others. I am pleased to recognize all Black changemakers, including my mentor Memphis Police **Captain Rufus J. Turner** (RIP). Hats off to his caring wife, **Mrs. Lucy Turner,** who encouraged me and others to "hang in there" since the first day we met.

Captain R.J. Turner

Black police officers often experienced intense pressure while proving they were fit for the job. Believe it or not, many were falsely blamed for over-policing to gain respect. Some were perceived to be more aggressive than the White officers. Some standout names were: Everidge C. "Shug" Jones, Ben

Whitney, William Moseley, and George "Top Cat" Small. Like others, these men were courageous police officers who shared a genuine concern for enforcing the rule of law.

Patrolman "Shug" Jones

A career that started nearly a half-century ago came to the closing chapter when Patrolman **Everidge C. "Shug" Jones** retired from the Memphis Police Department, March 24, 1964. Negroes were not allowed to work as patrolmen when Jones began working at the department. "Shug," as he is known, started with the department by doing odd jobs at the Police garage at 14. He can readily recall that those were the days for 'horses, and one electric patrol wagon used to transport prisoners.' Sixteen years ago, Jones and seven other Negro men became the first Negro policemen hired on the city force. Jones said, 'When I started with the department, I never dreamed that I would ever become a patrolman.' Jones said, 'When I started with the department, I worked in the garage, and I loved being a mechanic. I thought I would always be a garageman.' At that time, the Memphis Police department owned only one other automobile other than the patrol wagon, auto for the chief. However, there were horses and bicycles, which Jones also repaired. Jones said he installed the first radio used in a police car here. He explained how he invented a system employing a small pulley attached to the generator to prevent the radio from causing the battery to run down (Tri-State Defender [TSD], 1964).

Patrolman Jones and the other officers cleaned Beale Street,' of pimps, pickpockets, prostitutes, etc. Jones helped sponsor the first Negro Policeman's Ball here in Memphis. He told of shooting a man in the leg at S. Wellington St. and Georgia Ave. to prevent the man from shooting him after drawing a gun on him. Jones and his wife resided in Hyde Park, a North Memphis black neighborhood (TSD, 1964).

In Memphis, most Black police officers resided in the same neighborhood as the Black people they arrested. The neighborhood locations doubled their burden and required keen vigilance for the officers' family members and property.

Following retirement, Patrolman "Shug" Jones worked as a security officer at a department store in the Lamar-Airways shopping center. Reportedly, he died after suffering a heart attack while chasing a shoplifter fleeing from the department store. I pay homage to this Black trailblazer for his courage and respect for law and order.

THREE

Growing Up in South Memphis

"Lil Yarbro"

In the 1950s, I grew up in South Memphis around Mississippi Boulevard & Walker Avenue, near LeMoyne-Owen College, my alma mater, and the LeMoyne Gardens Housing Project. Other Black housing projects within a three-mile radius were the Fowler Homes, Foote Homes, and Cleaborn Homes.

Most of the elementary school kids in the area aspired to attend Booker T. Washington High School, home of the "Mighty Warriors." The marching band with the stepping majorettes was a spectacle to see. During the time, neighborhood school pride existed as a serious matter to Black youngsters throughout Memphis.

The intersection of Mississippi & Walker was commonly known as *"the Corner."* The iconic "ACE Theater" was the neighborhood place to go -- on *"the Corner"* -- for Black moviegoers and talent show fans. I can remember when the admission tickets were 10 and 25 cents each. The ACE Theater closed its doors for a brief period and later reopened with new owners as the RITZ Theater. The Black neighborhood movie business eventually fizzled out in Memphis.

As a boy, I was an enthusiastic fan of the amateur talent shows at the ACE Theater. The renowned Rufus Thomas and Robert "Bones" Crouch, a comic act, were the emcees. Many people remember when the Black amateur shows were at the Palace Theater on Beale Street and Handy Theater on Park Avenue in Orange Mound.

The South Memphis and Beale Street areas produced many amateur singers and musicians who later became famous recording stars. I saw local musical artists like William Bell, the Canes, the Del Rios, and Lewis Williams. Lewis

Williams became the lead singer for the Ovations, a hometown R&B singing group.

Mississippi & Walker was a flourishing small business and residential area continually busy with people, especially on weekends. Something exciting or unfortunate occurred every weekend on "the Corner."

I eye-witnessed disturbing police encounters on "the Corner," where Blacks endured abusive treatment without just cause. As boys, my friends and I never viewed White police officers as our friends. In our minds, we felt they treated all Black people as criminals or lawbreakers.

Black boys display anger about the frequency of stops by White police officers and their treatment during these stops. They view the officers as belligerent and antagonistic and are especially outraged by their use of racial slurs, profanity, and derogatory terms like "punk" and "sissy." They complain about police stops that are too often initiated by physical contact, such as grabbing, pushing, shoving, pulling, or tackling the youth to the ground (Davis & Henning, 2017).

In July 1950, my grandmother died when I was seven years of age. I moved in with Granddaddy and Lil Mama, my step-grandmother, at 975 Ford Place. Ford Place was the first street east of Walker Avenue, behind Yarbrough's Barber Shop at 1000 Mississippi Boulevard. The barbershop was next door to the historic Four-Way Grill, 998 Mississippi Boulevard, a world-known *Soul Food* restaurant owned by Mr. Clint and Mrs. Irene Cleaves. Mr. Clint was the chauffeur for E.H. "Boss" Crump, a former mayor and political powerbroker of Memphis, Tennessee.

Today, the "Four-Way Restaurant" remains open for business following new ownership and building renovation. Hats off to Patrice Bates Thompson, the proprietor. I rejoice when seated in the dining section once occupied by my granddaddy's barbershop.

My birth certificate showed that my mother named me after my granddaddy, Denver Yarbrough. My middle name appeared as Terry. Terry was the last name of my biological father, Hugh L. Terry. My mother and father never married. I used Denver Terry as a full name until the age of 23 when I applied to join the Memphis Police Department.

A Vital Records check discovered the correct full name I was required to use after changing my records. Wow, what a painstaking process that I do not wish on anybody. It had been unknown to me that my birth certificate was misplaced all those years. As a young boy, I remember Granddaddy telling Rosie Yarbrough, "I'll raise that boy. I don't want him to grow up and be a fool, spending his life in and out of jail."

Granddaddy had divorced my grandmother, Fannie Scott. He remarried in 1944 to Ersula Murphy, aka "Lil Mama," a beautician from Brownsville, Tennessee. My grandmother married again to Eugene "Mr. Gene" Scott. I was overly fond of Mr. Gene. I lived with Mr. Gene and grandmama Fannie until her death in July 1950.

When I moved in with Granddaddy and Lil Mama, they demanded that I respect authority, attend school, and attend church each Sunday. At the time, we worshipped at Central Baptist Church located on Mississippi Boulevard at Alston Avenue. Pastor Roy D. Morrison, Sr., was the senior pastor. Pastor Dr. Reuben H. Green, Sr., followed Reverend Morrison when he retired.

I attended Magnolia Elementary School in the first grade and LaRose Elementary School in the second through sixth grades. I hated to leave Magnolia because I became very fond of my first-grade teacher, Mrs. Chestine Cowan, a wonderful lady. We moved to 1260 Gill Avenue in the Hamilton High School district following the sixth grade at LaRose.

Starting with LaRose Elementary, Granddaddy visited my teachers each year to thank them and reinforce his parental support. He detested the thought of me not attending school, growing up partaking in lawlessness, and running from the police. Unlike many neighborhood boys, nothing of that sort was ever on my mind -- especially running from the police.

Granddaddy, born in 1903, always reminded me about his limited schooling as a boy growing up with his siblings on plantations around Red Banks and Byhalia, Mississippi. He made sure that I gave undivided attention when he talked about his family's challenging times.

Granddaddy reminded me, "Boy, I only have a fifth-grade education. I taught myself how to be a barber to make a living for my family and me. My daddy, mother, five brothers, three sisters, and I had to work on the White folks' plantations, farming, chopping, and picking cotton. We had to drop out of school to harvest the crops while the White folk's children attended school. That set us back; however, we made it by the grace of GOD Almighty. I will make sure you stay in school and get an education. Education is the main thing you need to make something out of yourself in life. Do you understand me?" I said, "Yes, sir."

I was a bashful young fellow who suffered a terrible speech impediment while growing up. Sometimes I stomped my foot to get a word out. However, I never allowed stuttering to stop me from interacting with my peers or anybody else. I admit there were many nervous times in the school classroom. I often knew the answers to teachers' questions but failed to respond because of my stuttering. I felt worthless and feared others would laugh and make fun of me. Sometimes I harbored evil thoughts when others laughed at me. My speech improved as I grew older. I discovered it was all about confidence and believing in yourself. I remained focused in life, not allowing my speech impediment to define me. I strived relentlessly to turn my impairment into a purpose.

Granddaddy insisted that I read the newspaper headlines and sports pages every day in the Commercial Appeal, a morning newspaper. That is how I became an avid Los Angeles Dodgers' baseball fan. I am incredibly grateful to Granddaddy for the tough-love teachings that influenced me to grow up to be like him.

He insisted that I learn how to work in the barbershop at the age of seven: shining shoes, cashiering, running errands, and doing custodial chores. The barbershop customers nicknamed me *Lil Yarbro*. At age 11, he allowed me to sell Tri-State Defender newspapers and JET magazines in the neighborhood. Both were popular Black-owned publications. This increased his trust in me and boosted my confidence in assuming responsibility.

Granddaddy's purpose was to teach me the importance of doing honest work, understanding the value of a dollar, and communicating with confidence. I remember several of his closest friends who were daily barbershop regulars: Mr. Morgan, a retired Illinois Central freight train engineer; Mr. Charlie Heiskell, our next-door neighbor; and Mr. Blocker, who owned a clean, black/white, 1953 Chevrolet he drove for over 20 years.

They sat laughing and talking for several hours on weekdays at the barbershop. I heard many arguments about preachers, politicians, prizefighters, and favorite baseball teams (Dodgers, Giants, Cardinals). It broke my heart to hear them talk about how Joe Louis, heavyweight champion, lost to Rocky Marciano. I idolized Joe Louis. I listened and became well informed on multiple barbershop subjects. I played asleep many times.

I will never forget the fundamental values learned from working at *Yarbrough's Barber Shop*. The values and teachings prepared me with self-discipline, common sense, and moral fortitude to survive adversity in life. Strangely, I never aspired to be a professional barber.

I never heard Granddaddy speak derogatorily about police officers other than when he mentioned how *"rotten"* some White police officers treated Black people in the South. He reminded me repeatedly to use common sense, do right, and stay out of their way. Granddaddy never gave me any reason to doubt his respect for law enforcement. He always respected authority and demanded that I do the same.

In summer 1955, I remember an occasion when two Mississippi police officers seriously upset Granddaddy. He had just purchased a new car, a 1955 Mercury Montclair, four-door, with a charcoal gray top and orange body.

One Sunday morning, Granddaddy decided to go to a childhood friend's funeral in Olive Branch, Mississippi, with a relative. I tagged along with them. We drove to the Halliburton Baptist Church for the funeral services. The cemetery was located directly behind the church building. On a hot Sunday before noon, people filled the church pews to pay their final respects to the deceased.

The lengthy funeral service was about to adjourn when two White police officers drove onto the front church grounds. They exited their patrol car, entered the church, and talked to an usher. An angry White passerby had complained that cars were double-parked in front of the church, partially blocking the roadway.

When the two officers left, Granddaddy asked an elderly man standing at the front door, "What did the police officers say?" The elderly man angrily said the police officers ordered the usher to tell the preacher, *"Hurry up and put that Nigger in the ground so we can get this road cleared out here."*

Everybody thought the two white officers disrespected the church and family of the deceased. While returning home, Granddaddy angrily expressed how some white people were still mistreating Black people in Mississippi. Many had no respect for Black churches whatsoever.

At the time, Emmitt Till, a 14-year-old Black boy from Chicago, was murdered by two white men in Money,

Mississippi. Emmitt was visiting his great uncle for the summer in 1955 when he allegedly whistled at a white woman while inside a store. Granddaddy predicted that Mississippi police officers' free-wheeling, racist behavior toward Black folk would never change in our lifetime.

****

Meanwhile, South Memphis was a densely populated high-crime area patrolled by White officers. Most of the White residents had started moving to East Memphis and the suburban areas. Black officers patrolling in cars did not exist in Memphis until the early 1960s. The first patrol car with Black officers was *"Car 15"*, assigned to the Orange Mound, Magnolia, Castalia Heights, and Dixie Heights areas. Black police officers could not physically arrest White citizens until 1963 or 1964. If needed, Black officers would detain white suspects at the scene before calling for white officers to make an arrest.

At any rate, police abuse on the streets was an everyday occurrence. Black males were continually stopped and harassed. Sometimes the harassing encounters were justified because of the loud cursing, gambling, and street fighting. Dice gaming appeared to be a common pastime behind the buildings around Mississippi & Walker.

It was funny to see the older men or boys run from the police, scattering like birds flying away from a fence. I admit they were their own worst enemy. Sadly, many of the dice arguments resulted in severe beatings or stabbings. The dice gaming hustle was a way of life for many of the younger men.

Four Black ambulance companies, Hayes, Qualls, Lewis, and Southern, were located within a three-mile radius of Mississippi & Walker, "*the Corner.*" Sometimes, it appeared they were racing to the scene to stake claim on an injured or deceased Black victim. Mr. Lewis, a one-arm driver, and his assistant often arrived first to claim and transport the victim to John Gaston Hospital. It amazed me to see how skillful Mr. Lewis maneuvered with one arm to secure a victim in the ambulance. Mr. Lewis was the owner of the R.S. Lewis Funeral Home on Vance Avenue.

Jack Ruby, a white ambulance company, was located on College Street at McLemore Avenue across from the Capitol Theater. The same theater building that later housed the famous STAX Recording Company. Jack Ruby's red ambulances did not respond to emergency calls to assist or transport Black victims. Racial segregation was at a peak in Memphis at the time.

White patrol officers would stop and call out to Black males, regardless of age, "*Come here, boy*" or "*Come here, Nigger, where are you going? We ought to get out of this car and beat your black ass.*" It was common knowledge that White officers rampantly beat Blacks on the streets with their nightsticks – especially at night. My friends and I viewed White police officers to be downright "lowdown" and disgusting.

I often heard older boys bragging that *"Running"* from the police was the right thing to do. They were afraid not to run because no one wanted to gamble on what the police officers might do to them. Fear was apparent because of the previous encounters with the white officers. Consequently, nobody wanted to go to jail. When a police car appeared, the innocent boys ran because the guilty boys ran.

Several White officers were known on the streets by their funny names, e.g., *"Baby Face"* and *"Red."* They often called Black boys to their patrol car to tell them, *"You Niggers go home, get off the streets, you black m-----f---ers!"* When the boys stepped back from the patrol car to walk away, an officer shouted, *"You Niggers better run, and you better run fast!"* Filing a complaint against White police officers was out of the question. Black citizens were too afraid. Police officials frequently ignored complaints from Black citizens.

Decades of data show that the journey to racial disparity begins when Black men are boys. Black boys were abused and carted to jail like no other demographic. They are policed on the street, in the mall, in school, in their homes, and on social media. Police stop Black boys on the vaguest of descriptions – "Black boys running," "two Black males in jeans, one in a gray hoodie," "Black male in athletic gear." Young black males are treated as if they are "out of place" when they are in white, middle-class neighborhoods and when hanging out in public spaces or sitting on their front porches. Black boys who congregate on the "corner" attract the attention of the police day or night. Even when they "dress nicely" or "drive nice cars," young Black males cannot avoid police surveillance since such signs of wealth among Black youth are presumed to be associated with drug dealing. Black boys describe their neighborhoods as overpoliced and say officers stop them multiple times a day to pat them down and ask questions like "Where are you coming from?" and "Where are you going?" Videotaping, cursing, ignoring an officer's orders, and running away provoke even greater hostility, disrespect, and often physical force from the police. Not surprisingly, Black boys are more likely to experience excessive force than white boys (Davis & Henning, 2017).

By the way, Granddaddy's barbershop was next door north of the *"Curve Pocket Billiards,"* a pool hall owned by Mr. Lucius *"Heavy"* Bolden. Mr. Bolden lived on Ford Place, too, across the street from our house. I often leaned on the corner of the Pool Hall's large front window to watch the men *"shoot pool"* at the first table. I was too young to go inside. Mr. Bolden or nobody else said anything to me because my name was *"Lil Yarbro,"* the little boy well-known from Mr. Yarbrough's barbershop. Mr. Bolden's pool hall was a thriving business at Mississippi & Walker; it stayed crowded on weekends.

In 1950-51, I remember when *J.B.'s Pool Hall* was booming, too, directly across the street next door to the ACE Theater. However, it eventually closed, and the Country Club Cafe opened later at the exact location. A short while after that, Lucky Strike Cleaners moved in on the corner next door to the cafe.

On weekends, several marked police cars often drove up in front of Mr. Bolden's pool hall. A group of White officers exited the vehicles and huddled as if to discuss a plan. Later, I learned that the police targeted Black pool halls, etc., for what they called *"Weapon Sweeps."*

When they entered the pool hall's front door, I saw and heard one officer shout out, *"Alright, you Niggers, put the sticks down, get your hands up, and face the wall! If you got anything on you, you better get rid of it before we get to you!"* The loud noise in the pool room suddenly stopped. Faintly, I could hear objects hitting the floor.

One officer stood at the front door to observe. The other officers searched the men, mostly retrieving pocketknives from the floor, putting them in cloth bags. They were rough while searching the men. Anyone found with a gun on them would be arrested and transported to jail. Watching the *"Weapons Sweep"* was a remarkable sight in Mr. Bolden's pool room. During those times, I learned that carrying a switchblade knife or straight razor was typical in ghetto areas. Both were usually carried in the zipper-fly of pants.

****

As a Hamilton High School ninth grader, I encountered two white police officers who deserved an academy award for their threatening nighttime scare tactics. Two friends and I worked at Leonard's Pit Barbecue; a popular, white-owned, drive-in restaurant located on Bellevue Boulevard at McLemore Avenue in South Memphis. We were "pickup boys," hired mainly to assist the male carhops, remove food trays from the customers' cars, and clean the parking lot after closing.

We always left work late after midnight. It was wiser and safer for the three of us to walk home together because we lived nearby. Leonard's Pit Barbecue Restaurant was my first job after I stopped working at Granddaddy's barbershop. I was a happy 15-year-old teenager earning money to purchase my school needs.

One weekend night, about 1:30 am, we walked home south on Bellevue when a police patrol car pulled alongside us at Bellevue Park. The White officer driving shouted, *"Where you Niggers coming from?"* I answered quickly, *"Sir, we're coming from work; we work at Leonard's Pit Barbecue down the street. We're going home, sir."* The driver shouted, again, *"What the f—k is Leonard's, Nigger? You mean Mr. Leonard's, don't you, Nigger!"* I said calmly, *"Yes, sir, I mean Mr. Leonard's."* The officer then faked as if he were exiting the car. Again, he shouted, *"You Niggers hurry up and get your black asses off the street."* I said, *"Yes, sir."* We left, walking fast.

Wow, we were afraid because the officer on the passenger side opened his door and stepped out quickly, pointing a long nightstick at us. *"Running"* would have been a foolish option for us. I will never forget the experience. As a result, it aroused my curiosity to consider a career in law enforcement. I would always ask myself, *"If I were to become a police officer, would I talk to and treat people like they were animals?"*

Well, nine years later, I became a Memphis police officer. It was an easy decision because of my motivation to help people and maintain gainful employment without a layoff.

March 4, 1968, I started my career with the Memphis Police Department (MPD).

January 9, 1984, I decided to resign from (MPD) in good standing for personal business, following 16 years of service.

August 12, 1985, the Shelby County Sheriff's Office (SCSO) hired me. Later, I earned three promotions to captain.

August 31, 2013, I retired from SCSO in good standing, following 28 years of service.

September 12, 2016 – February 21, 2019, I served as police chief at Mason, Tennessee.

FOUR

A New World of Reality

On March 4, 1968, I started work with the Memphis Police Department (MPD). On March 28, 1968, Dr. Martin Luther King, Jr. arrived in Memphis to lead a nonviolent march, promoting economic justice for the striking sanitation workers (Honey, 2018).

On February 12, 1968, about 1300 sanitation workers had gone on strike demanding union recognition, better working conditions, and higher wages. Mayor Henry Loeb and the City Council repeatedly refused their demands. Sanitation workers who suffered on welfare earned low wages, were paid no overtime for late hours, and relied on food stamps to feed their families (Brown, 2018).

Sadly, on April 4, 1968, Dr. King, Jr. was assassinated in Memphis the evening following his historic *"Mountain Top"* speech at Mason Temple. Dr. King's assassination sent shock waves through the city, the country, and around the world. Black people retaliated with violence around the country, breaking windows, looting, burning buildings, and setting vehicles afire (Conover, 2018).

In Memphis, Mayor Henry Loeb declared the city under martial law and imposed a nightly curfew. Loeb summoned help from the Tennessee Army National Guard and area law enforcement partners to stop the violence and maintain law and order (Brown, 2018).

At the time, Mayor Loeb's callous leadership style involving the Sanitation Workers helped fuel police abuse targeting Black citizens. The *"Us vs. Them"* policing mentality by White police officers was in full motion. Mayor Loeb became increasingly unyielding while refusing to honor any labor proposals by the sanitation workers and AFSCME union officials (Conover, 2018). The relentless Mayor and City Council created resentment and a broader divide between Black citizens and police officers. All indications showed that most Black citizens despised Mayor Loeb.

During the downtown march, violence suddenly erupted at the rear of the march. A group of young Black lawbreakers had disavowed Dr. King's nonviolent strategy by breaking windows and attempting to loot the stores. Memphis police officers moved in vigorously, severely beating the marchers with riot batons. As the marchers scattered in the Beale Street area, the police officers randomly stopped, brutally beat, and arrested innocent Black citizens (Odell Jr, 2020).

Several days before the march, I participated in a Ride-Along recruit training exercise approved by the Memphis Police Academy. Seven other Black trainees participated, too. We began the *"Ride-Along"* phase of recruit training as observers with designated patrol officers. The Ride-Along training was a realistic and exciting experience.

I had the opportunity to see and hear Mayor Henry Loeb speak to a large group of white police officers standing on the bed of a pickup truck in the parking lot at Armour Station. I stood out among those officers observing as a recruit trainee. Mayor Loeb answered questions, demanded law and order, and warned the officers about "outside agitators" coming to Memphis.

Mayor Loeb reinforced his firm objections regarding the striking sanitation workers and the AFSCME labor union. I watched the White officers blurt out disparaging remarks and racial slurs berating Dr. King. News reports had indicated Dr. King would be returning to Memphis to lead a big march. It was challenging for me to stand there and listen to the officers berate Dr. King. Dr. King represented the same human values that I sought to gain and protect.

There I stood stunned, as a Black recruit trainee, watching my future partners and coworkers act foolishly. Believe it or not, I was naïve enough to think that Dr. Martin Luther King, Jr, was well-liked by everybody. I quickly realized a new world of reality was staring me in the eyes. And I could not do anything about it — but adjust. Did I want this job or not? Yes, I chose to stay and try to make a difference.

In June 1968, following graduation from the Memphis Police Academy, I reported to the Memphis City Jail, 128 Adams, for my first duty assignment. This experience began a new world of reality for me. What an eye-opening and learning experience for rookie police officers.

After four months, I was one of four Black officers transferred to Armour Station in East Memphis to integrate the patrol cars further. No doubt, the white officers resented our presence. However, they accepted us without displaying any life-threatening hostility. As newcomers, we expected the usual silent treatment, bitterness, and mind games played by white officers. We eagerly adjusted to our probation period to earn satisfactory performance evaluations from our supervisors.

Later, on-duty, I experienced appalling encounters with coworkers as I adjusted to a *new world of reality*. I dreaded reporting to roll call on many occasions. However, the racial jokes heard about Dr. King, Maxine Smith, and other activists motivated me to stay focused and learn my job.

I received a regular assignment to Car 14 with two veteran white partners. Car 14's ward included the Orange Mound community, from Park Avenue on the South to Poplar Avenue on the north, bordered by Greer Street on the east and East Parkway on the west. Later, Car 40, deployed as a backup unit to Car 14. Orange Mound enjoyed the distinction as one of the oldest Black communities in the state of Tennessee.

The training officers knew all aspects of the job very well. I encountered no problems passing my probationary period and adjusting to my regular partners. Sometimes, I was not too fond of their indifferent attitudes when interacting with Black citizens. However, I focused on maintaining effectiveness and learning the streets in my ward. I enjoyed more positive experiences than negative ones.

As previously mentioned, I was not a radical or a racist by any stretch of one's imagination. I harbored no hate or ill-will toward any of my partners. I highly valued the mutual respect and trust we shared. Today, I am deeply grateful for the friendships acquired while working as a Memphis police officer.

****

Meanwhile, I remember Memphis city court hearings as a spectacle to behold. No doubt, Black spectators outnumbered Whites attending city court. It appeared as if White police officers disproportionately ticketed and arrested Black citizens, overlooking most White lawbreakers for unknown reasons. I believe Blacks represented about 95% of the crowded courtrooms.

The city of Memphis demographics showed White residents to outnumber Black residents. Today, according to U.S. Census records, Black residents outnumber White residents in Memphis. The crowded city court attendance remains about the same for Black citizens at the Criminal Justice Center, 201 Poplar Avenue.

Attorneys and Bail Bond agents crowded the hallway areas of City Court, at 128 Adams, conferring with clients and out-of-custody defendants. It was disgusting to see and hear how White attorneys hustled their poor Black clients in the hallway. White attorneys were heard saying, *"Bring me some more money in two weeks, so I can get your case continued."* This tactic was unprofessional and unethical. It appeared as no consequence to the attorneys since their clients were Black.

The crafty attorneys knew full well that their poor Black clients did not have the money. Likely, their clients would commit more crimes to get the money. They did just that, resulting in a disgusting cycle of hopelessness for the poor client. *"Going to court"* was a regular ritual for many Black clients. Even if they were not on the court docket, young Black spectators felt it was stylish to attend court to see, *"Who copped a case and got locked up."*

During the early 1970s, we knew one City Court judge as a favorite among Black citizens because of his demeanor toward Blacks, compared to other judges. When testifying in City Court, police officers referred to Black *"defendants"* as *"subjects."* White officers never enunciated the word *"Negro"* correctly. They intentionally pronounced the word *"Negro"* as *"Nigra"*, e.g., *"male Nigra"* or *"female Nigra."*

At the time, police officers commonly referred to Blacks as *"male Colored"* or *"female Colored"* in police reports and court testimony. The standard race categories are Black, White, Asian, American Indian or Alaska Native, Native Hawaiian, or Other Pacific Islander. The ethnicity categories are Hispanic or Latino and Not Hispanic or Latino.

During a crowded court session, the favorite Judge halted a White officer's testimony and ordered all police officers to stop referring to Black *"defendants"* as *"subjects"* in his courtroom. He emphasized that saying *"male Nigra subject"* or *"female Nigra subject"* was improper.

The Judge required immediate compliance to his order without any exceptions. He further ordered police officers appearing in his courtroom to refer to individuals listed on the court docket by the term *"defendant."* The Judge's verbal order eventually became a best practice for all city courtrooms.

****

As a rookie patrolman on probation, my regular partners reminded me that I needed to throw away that *"little nightstick"* issued by the Academy. They mocked my nightstick as a *"toothpick"* and demanded that I get a larger one, *"So, I could do some damage if I had to use it."* My partners were adamant about *"cracking heads"* if they had to do it, suggesting I do the same.

Their nightsticks were about two feet long and two and one-half inches thick. Years later, the Memphis Police Department issued a written policy to govern the terminology, use, and type of batons and impact weapons allowed. A Memphis furniture manufacturer donated the thick nightsticks to police officers as appreciation for their service.

I cooperated with my partners; however, I never used my nightstick to *"knock"* or *"crack"* anybody's head. I never aspired to be known as a brutal police officer. However, I did what I had to do to protect myself effectively and do my job. White officers joked about how delighted they were to testify in

Court standing next to a *"Nigra"* defendant wearing a *"John Gaston turban."* White tape and gauze heavily covered the Black defendant's head resembling a white skull cap. I found the white officers' jokes about cracking heads to be appalling and indeed not funny.

The following explains how the term *"John Gaston turban"* originated.

In 1968, Claude Armour was the Commissioner of Memphis Fire & Police. Maxine Smith was the Executive Secretary of the Memphis Branch of the NAACP.

However, under Armour's stewardship of the department, allegations of police misconduct against African Americans did not cease. Maxine Smith accused the department of arresting Blacks without cause in some instances and mistreating them. Smith said, *"Police officers can do whatever they want to do under the guise of being police officers."* The term *"John Gaston turban"* originated among the city's defense lawyers. It referenced the many swaddled Blacks' heads beaten by police and treated at the public John Gaston Hospital. Young blacks had another term for police violence: Blue Crush (Rosenbloom, 2018).

My first rookie encounter with coworkers involved an

attempted vehicle stop by two White officers operating Car 19, a dayshift patrol unit. I was in uniform driving to work when I noticed blue lights flashing behind me about three blocks from Armour Station. The officers had trailed me a few blocks aware of my identity and destination.

I chose not to stop to avoid being late for roll call. When I parked and exited my vehicle, the driver pulled up and asked, *"Didn't you see the damn blue lights flashing behind you?"* I said, *"Yes, but I was not aware of any violation I committed. Plus, I cannot be late for roll call."* The officer yelled, *"Next time, you make damn sure you stop, you understand."* In disgust, I said nothing. I walked away and entered the building.

Following roll call, I met with the lieutenant and Captain to vent my frustration. The captain instructed me to write a memo of complaint about the incident. I submitted my written complaint to the captain, however, to no avail. To no surprise, the captain never discussed the written complaint with me.

****

The second encounter involved a conversation I had with a White lieutenant during a routine meeting in the field. The lieutenant met with my partner and me to collect offense reports and traffic citations. We met with him on the Krystal Drive-In parking lot at Poplar & Greer across the street from East High School. We met regularly at Krystal's to drink coffee and update our lieutenant on calls and activity details.

Before meeting us, the lieutenant had responded to the

Memphis State University campus and Highland Street area to monitor a sit-in protest at Memphis State. Maxine Smith, the local NAACP president, and Black Student Association members were staging a sit-in at the president's office. The peaceful protest had attracted public attention and the news media.

During our conversation, I asked, *"Lieutenant, were there any problems at the Memphis State sit-in protest?"* He replied firmly, *"Well, Yarbrough, no reflection on you! Maxine Smith and the other Niggers, they just over there acting like a bunch of crazy-ass Niggers!"* The lieutenant felt comfortable expressing himself to me in the manner he did, or he did not care.

I displayed no spontaneous reaction and gave no reason for him to think I was upset. The lieutenant's disgust involved the following school organization:

"The Black Student Association at Memphis State University was formed in 1967 to improve the quality of campus life for Black students, provide networking and social activities, and help organize student actions" (Bradley, 2019).

April 1969, Black students staged a sit-in in the office of university president Cecil Humphreys. They protested the school not being fully integrated and asked why Humphreys denied funding to bring Congressman Adam Clayton Powell, Jr. -- an outspoken proponent of the Black Power Movement - - to speak at the Black Student Association's upcoming Black Extravaganza program. Six White students and 103 Black students were arrested (Bradley, 2019).

As a rookie, I was taken aback with no apparent recourse other than *"hear and don't hear."* The lieutenant's lousy attitude and unkind words certainly did not stop the mission or impede the protesters' progress on Memphis State University's campus.

****

On another occasion, while parked at Krystal's, my partner and I drank a cup of coffee when a Memphis Police traffic unit drove up with two white officers. The marked *"black and white"* car pulled the driver's side to my passenger side, where I was sitting. At the time, Traffic Division cars were white with black hoods. All other Memphis Police patrol units were black with gold reflective lettering.

The passenger officer yelled to my partner who was driving, *"Hey, I hear y'all got some 'spots' in the roll call out there. They told me it's about three or four of them."* The officer ignored me altogether. He looked across me and talked directly to my partner, sitting at the steering wheel with both pant legs pulled up to his knees. I noticed that my partner regularly drove this way as a habit. He had strange driving habits.

My partner dared to yell across me, *"Naw, it's not four; it's just three of them. They ain't worth a sh-t either. We got to put up with them."* As they rambled on with their so-called joking, I looked at my partner, unappreciative of his responses. Because he certainly was talking like a fool. I started to say something at one point; I just shrugged it off as if they said nothing. I believe they were testing my reaction to their stupid comments.

****

A most embarrassing situation occurred as my partner, and I answered a complaint call in the Orange Mound "Beltline" neighborhood near Southern Avenue and Boston Street. The elderly female complainant's small frame house was in an impoverished Black area. However, I was impressed with the neat appearance of the home on the inside. While meeting with the complainant, my partner and I remained in the small living room. She and relatives gathered around to explain the complaint situation to us.

There was a makeshift coffee table in front of the sofa built with stacked wooden beverage cases. As my partner listened to the complainant, he rested his right foot on the corner of the table. The relatives immediately stared at me to tell him to take his foot off their table. My partner leaned forward on the table as if to add insult to injury and crossed both forearms on his right knee. He maintained that position for about five minutes while listening and talking to the complainant.

The question is, *"Do I believe my partner would have placed his foot atop a coffee table in a White complainant's home?"* The answer is, *"Absolutely not."* He showed no respect for the Black complainant's house because of the poor neighborhood. Simply, he did not care. My partner returned to the patrol unit degrading the residents and area. Again, as a rookie, I shrugged it off and did not respond to him because of his *"senior officer"* status.

I burned out after three years of patrolling the Orange Mound, Hollywood, and Douglas neighborhoods. Fortunately, I succeeded with my transfer to the Community Relations Bureau. My volunteer work in Community Relations had sparked my genuine interest in police-community programs.

FIVE

My Philosophy: How It Started

During the 1970s, *"Police Community Relations"* was a policing philosophy adopted with mutual trust and cooperation between the Memphis Police Department and law-abiding Black citizens. The winning philosophy promoted an initiative-taking concept to build trust, establish partnerships, and deter crime with workable solutions and best practices. I became attracted to this initiative-taking concept known today as *"Community Policing."*

Years later, I credited former Police Director Toney Armstrong for revitalizing *"Community Policing"* in Memphis. I viewed Director Armstrong's policing philosophy as most suitable for deterring crime with community action partnerships.

Former Police Director Frank Holloman first implemented a Community Relations model in Memphis around 1969-70, to calm racial tension. Immediately after Dr. Martin Luther King's assassination, a retaliatory, riotous uprising erupted in the inner-city destroying property to the detriment of public safety. Rampant rumors loomed creating massive distrust and alleging suspicious circumstances involving the Memphis Police and Dr. King's death.

Police *"Service Centers"* were later opened in six designated high-crime neighborhoods to establish partnerships and promote mutual trust with community programs. The centers were manned by police officers assigned to the Community Relations Bureau headed by Lieutenant R.J. Turner. Those officers collaborated with community stakeholders to coordinate projects, resolve issues, and deter crime.

I believe Director Holloman, a retired FBI agent, knew Dr. King's assassination was not a good image of national and world fame for Memphis. The "Bluff City" had begun to emerge with increased popularity for the wrong reason. However, Director Holloman's community plan thrived with Lieutenant Turner in charge of operations.

Notable police officers assigned to the Community Relations Bureau were Bob Ferguson, R. Felix, Downing Newman, Ed Redditt, Herman Seaborn, Phil Burkhalter, James Ivy, O. Bradberry, Ben Whitney, Jan Moore, Michael Sims, Carl Mister, Roger Prewitt, Harrell Ray, Howard Terry, and Robert Ewing.

I certainly would be remiss if I neglected to recognize Mrs. Elnora Short, a dedicated volunteer. Mrs. Short was eventually hired as a civilian employee at Police Service Center #2 on Florida Street until it closed. Mrs. Short remained with the police department in a support services capacity.

Also, I am pleased to recognize Mr. Clarence Stewart, a civilian, for his outstanding volunteer service as the baseball coach at Center #2.

The Community Relations model downsized in the mid-1970s after the Black community's riotous retaliation to Elton Hayes' death on October 15, 1971. Hayes was a seventeen-year-old Black teenager who Memphis police officers and Shelby County deputy sheriffs allegedly beat to death after a high-speed pickup truck chase (Vecsey, 1971). Hayes' death captured national attention.

The Black community became enraged over a disputed police report that Hayes died from injuries after being thrown from the speeding pickup truck. The report indicated the driver lost control and crashed in the exit ramp off the expressway. Hayes was one of three young occupants in the pickup truck driven by his friend. The police report sparked racial tension and an orderly protest march within the inner city (Vecsey, 1971).

I recalled the outgoing Mayor Henry Loeb imposing a curfew in Memphis and calling on the Tennessee Army National Guard to help stamp out the violence. The sporadic violence involved rock-throwing, breaking windows, looting, and setting fires, as reported by citizens.

At Armour Station roll calls, I heard White officers joke about *"stirring it up in the streets"* to keep the action and overtime pay going. Those misguided officers viewed the curfew and riotous disorder as an opportunity to create overtime and make more money. Rumors were afloat that police officers committed much vandalism during the curfew to prolong the working hours.

In the Hayes case, the Shelby County grand jury returned indictments on the at-scene police officers for first-degree murder and assault to murder. On December 6, 1973, news reports indicated that an all-male jury of nine white men and three black men found eight law officers not guilty of the charges (Darnell, 1973). According to a New York Times article, the Shelby County District Attorney expected the indictments returned due to the conflicting at-scene evidence (Vecsey, 1971).

The Memphis Police Community Relations Bureau discontinued its programs due to budget constraints or lack of interest by the police director and executive command. However, the Police Amateur Boxing Program managed to survive, thanks to a partnership with the Memphis Housing Authority (MHA). MHA donated building accommodations in Lauderdale Courts Housing Project for a Community Relations HQ, 264 N. Lauderdale, and a Police Amateur Boxing Gym, 243 Winchester.

During the early 1980s, Sheriff's Office deputies Randy Wade, Joe Ball, and Melvin Shipp spearheaded community relations programs in unincorporated county areas.

Allow me to explain how I became interested in Memphis Police community relations and how it affected my policing philosophy. Please understand that my interest in community relations did not disparage the Memphis Police role in apprehending criminals or maintaining law and order. I always believed that criminals and lawbreakers must be held accountable for their wrongdoings with certainty.

However, I eventually realized that the criminal justice system did not operate on a level playing field for Black citizens, particularly young males. Excessive force, botched investigations, wrongful convictions, and disproportionate incarceration -- influenced by race and systemic racism -- have ruined the lives of too many innocent people.

Police departments must share responsibility with communities to deter crime and lawlessness, addressing issues with workable solutions. I was genuinely committed to contributing beyond my call of duty as a Black police officer. I became assertive in adopting a community policing philosophy I discovered was the right thing for me to do.

As a patrol officer, I focused on creative ways to discourage neighborhood crime and lawlessness by targeting disadvantaged boys with athletic and cultural enrichment programs. I often engaged teenage boys with street conversations encouraging them to avoid ruining their lives with crime and incarceration. So many were prone to trouble, loitering, and wasting time with nothing constructively in mind. It was personally satisfying to steer young boys in the right direction away from crime and lawlessness.

I convinced many boys to get involved in the Memphis Police youth baseball league and amateur boxing programs. I explained how I regularly assisted with those programs representing the Police Service Center #1 at Mississippi and Trigg Avenue. Some accepted my offer and successfully participated, eventually changing their negative opinions of police officers. The positive relationships we established with the boys reinforced our program objectives and increased their desire to become productive citizens.

The 1973 "Orioles" baseball team represented Police Service Center #1 as one of six teams in the **Police-WDIA Summer Youth Baseball League.** This group of boys, 13–15 years old, hailed from LeMoyne Gardens, Foote Homes, and Cleaborn Homes. Some standouts were **Donald *"Crumpy"* Crump, David McNeil, Barry Collier, and Wayne Mays.** How can we forget **Ronald and Donald Boyd,** twin brothers from LeMoyne Gardens? Their brother, **Harold Boyd,** was my reliable contact in helping to mentor the team. **Winston Ford** was another top baseball standout from the Riverside-Carver area. Ford, too, later became a Memphis police officer. Hats off to all participants in our Baseball and Touch Football programs at Service Center #1. Some South Memphis neighborhoods represented were Riverside, Montgomery Plaza (West Parkway-Florida areas), Tulane Apartments, and Magnolia-Castalia areas.

Orioles 1972-1973

Memphis Police - WDIA Youth Baseball League

One summer day, I visited the home of Mr. Harry T. Cash, my former principal at Hamilton High School. I had seen him the previous week judging amateur boxing bouts at the Fairgrounds Pipkin Building. Luckily, I found Mr. Cash working in his spacious basement once utilized as an amateur boxing gym.

During my visit, Mr. Cash asked how I was doing as a Memphis police officer. Mr. Cash's telephone call to Chief J.C. McDonald helped me to enroll in the Memphis Police Academy on March 4, 1968. I am forever grateful to Mr. Cash for his support and guidance. I explained to Mr. Cash my interest in transferring from my uniform patrol assignment to the community relations bureau. He praised my transfer effort because he recognized my passion for community service.

Interestingly, Mr. Cash reminded me how involved the Memphis Police Department and Sheriff's Office were with their youth boxing programs. He explained that amateur boxing was a great individual sport for coaching and mentoring wayward boys. Boxing required self-discipline, strenuous preparation, and good sportsmanship to accomplish winning outcomes. I was focused and energized to encourage Black boys to become productive citizens, not criminals.

Mr. Cash shared his longtime experience of training Black boxers and maintaining a boxing gym in the basement of his home. He and his associates sponsored the Tri-State Amateur Boxing Tournament at Church Park Center in Memphis for years. The event supported the Cynthia Milk Fund, a local charity for small children.

The local Tri-State tournament allowed Black amateur boxers to advance to regional and national competitions during segregated times. Black fighters were unable to compete against White boxers in Memphis at the time. Black boxers found other avenues to compete and advance to the National Golden Gloves Tournament. *"In 1958, eight Negro boxers from Memphis, TN, made up the Golden Gloves team representing Paducah, KY. The team competed in the Chicago Golden Gloves Tournament. This was the road to the big times"* (Jones, 2021).

Most of Mr. Cash's amateur boxers became champions in the ring and accomplished citizens out of the ring. For example, **Dr. Brown McGhee** (RIP) earned an NCAA Boxing Scholarship to the University of Wisconsin. McGhee received his undergraduate degree from the University of Wisconsin and later became a medical trauma physician. Afterwards, the NCAA discontinued sanctioning the sport of boxing for collegiate competition. **Dr. Willie W. Herenton** received his undergraduate degree from LeMoyne Owen College and later became the Superintendent of Memphis City Schools and the Honorable Mayor of Memphis, TN, for 18 years.

Several local Black amateur boxers I remember as a young boy were Brown McGhee, Ernest Buford, Willie *"Duke"* Herenton, Joe Willie DeMyers, Gerald Moore, Alfred Moore, Ernest Lanier, Harry Lanier, Cecil Boyd, Ulysses Moore, Thomas Bell, Willie Bell, Harry Manning, Tommie Johnson, Clayton Palmore, Clinton Palmore, and Aaron Hackett. Later, in 1970, I met Earl Wilson and Nathaniel *"Nate"* Jackson. In 1970, Nate Jackson was crowned the National AAU Light Heavyweight Champion.

I informed Mr. Cash I never boxed, but I liked to watch the sport of boxing. He shared with me how to work out and learn the basic punching and fundamental techniques of boxing. Once I started working out, I learned quickly and began showing others as I improved.

Before transferring to the Community Relations Bureau, fellow officers who mocked my decision asked, *"Yarbrough, you are crazy; why the hell do you want to go there? Do you know that is not policing? That is a social worker's job. You will never get promoted over there."* I told them that remained to be seen. Most of my fellow officers felt the Community Relations assignment was not adventurous enough for them and was not the job for a police officer. I told them that, *"I beg to differ; you do your thing, and I will do mine."* I kept stepping with no regrets. Thanks to Lieutenant R.J. Turner, the Community Relations Bureau afforded me a grand opportunity to *"protect and serve"* in a much broader sense.

Following my transfer, my new assignment started at Police Service Center #1, 1277 Mississippi Boulevard, in South Memphis. I worked with **Officer Carl Mister** (RIP), who I knew from Hamilton High School. Mister retired with the rank of Captain. Carl Mister and I worked closely together and were surprisingly successful with our neighborhood involvement programs.

We engaged the community with various projects: The South Memphis Law & Order Civic Club, Memphis Referral Center, Memphis Public Library Outreach, Food & Clothing

Assistance, Youth School Dances, Speaking Engagements, Police-WDIA Summer League Baseball, Youth Touch Football, and the South Memphis Boxing Bees.

Memphis Police amateur boxing became a flourishing community relations program where we impacted the lives of countless disadvantaged boys. The program was one of several sanctioned by the Memphis Amateur Boxing Association (MABA). I commend the leadership and coordination provided by Lieutenant Bob Ferguson, Sergeant D.S. Newman, and Lieutenant Alex McCollum.

Mister and I traveled the regional and national circuit as the qualifying boxers competed and advanced in the competition. Some top amateur tournaments were: Mid-South Golden Gloves, Southeastern AAU, Amateur Boxing Federation (ABF), Junior Olympics, Bill Cummings (USABA) Ohio State Fair Championships, and National Police Athletic League (PAL) Championships.

Special thanks to Bevo Covington, Herman Holeyfield, Joey Hadley, Red Fortner, Leo Miller, James House, Bill Lanier, Elias Tate, Bennie Thomas, Cecil Boyd, Clay Huddleston, Sr., Chester Kirkendoll, Willie Joe Alexander, Don Tilillie, and Carl Mister for mentoring young men to be character winners and productive citizens. I commend the MABA members, referees, judges, medical doctors, ring announcers, glovers, volunteer coaches, and supporting fans for the success of amateur boxing in Memphis.

In August 1973, the Community Relations staff was incredibly grateful to renowned **singer Al Green** for his Mid-South Coliseum Benefit Show that netted a $25,000 donation to the Citizens-Police Community Relations Committee. Al Green's generosity was most helpful to sustaining police-community relations programs.

1979 Memphis AAU Boxing Champions

I will never forget the summer day in 1976 when Muhammad Ali, world heavyweight boxing champion, visited the Memphis Police Boxing Gym unannounced in Lauderdale Courts. Ali pulled off his shirt at the front entrance, started shadow boxing, and loudly challenged anybody to the ring. What a sight it was to behold. I could not believe my eyes.

James Dixon, a local heavyweight, accepted the fun challenge, gloved up, and entered the boxing ring with Ali. Ali danced around Dixon like a buzz-saw, jabbing his head and talking trash to the delight of the audience. Ali kept repeating his trash talk, *"I'm floating like a butterfly, stinging like a bee... Now you see me, and now you don't."*

Muhammad Ali's visit was one I will treasure forever. Ali stopped by the Police Boxing Gym after visiting the young patients at St. Jude Children's Research Hospital, across the street from the gym.

The following familiarizes readers with how Muhammad Ali started in amateur boxing. As a 12-year-old boy, Cassius Clay (Muhammad Ali) developed an endearing relationship with Joe E. Martin, a White police officer in Louisville, Kentucky.

Officer Joe Martin & Cassius Clay

In 1954, Cassius Clay, 12-years old, reportedly met Joe Elsby Martin, a Louisville, Kentucky, white police officer who ran a local recreation center called the Columbia Gym for black and white amateur boxers. Young Cassius Clay sought Officer Martin to report that his new Schwinn bicycle, a gift from his father, had been stolen. Driven by anger, Cassius was anxious to locate the thief to beat him up.

Martin calmly quelled Cassius's anger by convincing him to sign-up at his boxing gym and learn how to fight to avoid trouble for street fighting. Cassius fell in love with Martin's advice and the boxing gym. Little did they know, this positive relationship between a police officer and a Black angry kid would develop into a world heavyweight boxing phenomenon.

The boxing lessons patrolman Joe Martin imparted to the young Cassius Clay retain their symbolic punch more than 60 years later. With the national PAL (Police Athletic League) in discussions to form a Louisville chapter, the story of a policeman reaching across the racial divide of a segregated city to help a young boy channel his anger over a stolen bicycle is worth retelling and a worthy foundation on which to build (Sullivan, 2020).

Officer Joe Martin bonded with Cassius and trained him at his local recreation center. The relationship helped launch an amateur boxing career that led Cassius to become a 1960 United States Summer Olympics light-heavyweight gold medalist.

Officer Martin successfully channeled Cassius's anger from the streets to becoming a law-abiding teenager, renowned heavyweight boxing champion, humanitarian, human rights activist, and controversial celebrity. In 1964, Cassius Clay became known as Muhammad Ali; the rest is history. Joe E. Martin, one of many good, honorable White police officers across the country, passed away at the age of 80 in 1996.

This story rebukes the false assumptions and warped opinions of misguided police officers who believe community-oriented policing programs are a waste of time and taxpayers' dollars. Also, it helps confirm that all White police officers are not "Bad Apples."

Ironically, I became a Memphis police officer assigned to patrol predominately Black, high-crime areas like Orange Mound, Hollywood & Douglas, and Binghampton. As a rookie, I had worked at the City Jail for about five months before completing my Uniform Patrol probationary period. The Jail experience had enlightened me to a new world of reality.

After a year and six months, I began patrolling and interacting with at-risk Black boys in those underserved neighborhoods. At that point, I had started to work as a volunteer in the MPD amateur boxing program, at Police Service Center #1, in South Memphis.

Whenever possible, I felt a need to stop on the streets and try to reason with some of the boys I tagged as destined for big trouble. I wanted to gain their confidence and try convincing them to avoid the lure and appetite for crime and lawlessness. Instead, pride themselves on staying in school and becoming productive citizens. However, some of my White partners were reluctant; they felt I wasted time and talked in vain. Guess what? Strangely, several were the same misguided white officers who resented my Black presence when I transferred to Uniform Patrol in East Memphis.

I discovered that Police amateur boxing programs were rewarding to mentor at-risk boys in underserved urban areas. Amateur boxing was an ideal individual sport for the boys to showcase physical prowess and channel energy in the right direction. In addition, I stressed character building, respecting law and order, and changing unwarranted opinions about police officers.

Most Black boys viewed White police officers as their enemy, the same as I thought as a young boy. Their street interactions with the police were usually negative. I eventually learned that many boys were anxious for a mere opportunity to be mentored, appreciated, and accepted as worthy human beings. However, I made no excuses for those who resorted to bad choices, violated laws, and defied police authority. They clearly understood that I meant business and did not condone any wrongdoing whatsoever.

Little did I know that one day I would be advocating for community-oriented policing after witnessing, as a young boy, White police officers arbitrarily abusing Black people. Contrary to biased opinions, police-community programs help to build positive relationships and change negative attitudes. Subsequently, full-time police-community relations officers are an asset to building trust and sustaining positive relationships.

Too often, community relations officers are frowned upon by fellow police officers and labeled as social workers. Many are subjected to scathing criticism from misguided peers who are indifferent to urban programs benefiting majority-Black residents. In my opinion, community relations officers are unsung heroes impacting lives, changing attitudes, and addressing crime issues with collaborative initiatives and solutions.

****

My good friend, Bevo Covington (RIP), operated the Memphis Park Commission's amateur boxing program with the same goals and objectives as the Memphis Police program. We partnered to build character and impart discipline to develop productive citizens with the sport of amateur boxing. Bevo Covington coached and mentored **Kennedy McKinney** as a young amateur boxer in Memphis, Tennessee. McKinney became the 1988 United States Summer Olympics bantamweight gold medalist. We all were incredibly proud of McKinney.

KENNEDY McKINNEY
1988 United States Summer Olympics
Bantamweight Gold Medalist - Seoul, Korea

Outstanding Memphis Park Commission amateur champions coached by Bevo Covington were Kelvin Bowen, McKinney's brother; Walter Ivory, Vertel Culp, Tony Rosser, Kenny Cole, Herschel Cole, Michael Herron, John House, Elvin Evans, and Clay Huddleston, Jr. There were others not listed.

Outstanding Memphis Police amateur champions were Johnny Rhodes, Michael Smith, Elias Tate, John Turner, Clarence Gilmore, Arnell Thomas, Howard Davis, Jr., Harvey Vaughn, Richard Dawson, Donald Johnson, Dock Gray, Willie Pollard, Michael Lawson, William Washington, Rusty Skidmore, Willis Ealy, Wilbert *"Honeycomb"* Blaine, Craig Wright, Leon Miller, Willie Burnett, Ray Burnett, Carl Burnett, Percy Reed, Allen Reed, Ed Pollard, Derek Payne, Pee-Wee Payne, Avery Braden, Eric Williamson, and Derrick Williamson. Several unknown names are not listed.

A Citizens-Police Community Relations Committee comprised of Memphis business executives met monthly to provide business and financial oversight for the Community Relations Bureau. The Memphis Police Department was obligated to provide personnel, salaries, vehicles, travel expenses, materials, and supplies. The Police Department did not control the contributions received from any of the donors, monetary or otherwise.

Meantime, I resigned from the Memphis Police Department in January 1984 and joined the Shelby County Sheriff's Office in August 1985. Thanks to former Sheriff Gene Barksdale, I was accepted into the Sheriff's Training Academy without delay. I worked for Sheriff Barksdale when he was an Inspector with the Memphis Police Department, commanding the Public Relations and Community Relations Bureaus.

In 1973, Inspector Barksdale approved my written proposal recommending that renowned singer Al Green do a benefit show to support Memphis Police community programs. Inspector Barksdale and group met with Al Green at his Winchester Road office to secure and welcome the benefit show. In August 1973, Al Green and supporting artists successfully performed before a capacity crowd of 10,000 or more at the Mid-South Coliseum.

Several of my coworkers were skeptical that my proposal would not work. As an Al Green fan, I was already familiar with his incredible talent and growing popularity rated by the Billboard Magazine R&B & Pop charts. I remember one of my White coworkers, a sergeant, looked over the large coliseum crowd and said, *"Yarbrough, I eat my words; your idea made it happen."* The show was a whopping success and an excellent benefit to sustaining police-community programs.

In August 1985, I switched to the Shelby County Sheriff's Office (SCSO) after 16 years of service with the Memphis Police Department (MPD). I opted for a fresh start in law enforcement after resigning from MPD in January 1984 to set up a business I closed about 18 months later. The Sheriff's Academy training experience was a rigorous challenge for me. However, I completed the academy in tip-top physical condition.

Memphis Police officials had denied my request for a leave of absence, prompting me to step away on faith with high hopes of returning. The Chief Inspector with command oversight of my bureau assured me that I could return with no problem. He praised my good employment record.

However, when I attempted to return after one year, City Personnel officials required me to reapply. I became distraught and refused to do so. I decided to move on to another agency for a fresh start.

As a young Memphis police officer, I had boasted that the skills of city police officers were a cut above those of county deputy sheriffs. At the time, city officers commonly referred to deputy sheriffs as the *"country"* police. I learned later that was the farthest thing from the truth.

Comparatively, I found the Sheriff's Office more political than the Memphis Police Department. The Sheriff was an independently elected official accountable to the people who elected them. Sheriffs do not follow a chain of command specific to their organization.

When a Sheriff's authority is abused by deputy sheriffs who demonstrate racial bias, the equal rights of minorities are likely jeopardized to favor the majority. The Sheriff of Shelby County is accountable to the County Board of Commissioners for budget funding at all departmental levels. The Tennessee Constitution governs the powers, duties, and responsibilities of the office of Sheriff. I found that a Sheriff's administrative, patrol, traffic, and investigative functions are operationally identical to a police department.

The Sheriff of Shelby County is responsible for securing county jail inmates and enforcing the rule of law within unincorporated patrol areas beyond city limits. Additional functions included the General Investigations Bureau, Fugitive

Division, Civil Division, Court Security & Operations, Reserve and Emergency Services Division.

I am proud of my 28 years of service with the Shelby County Sheriff's Office. The most memorable time spent was the 11 years I contributed as a Training Academy instructor. I cherished recruit basic training and contributing to the professional development of veteran law enforcement officers.

I am deeply grateful to **Sergeant Roosevelt Moore (Ret.), former Deputy Ron Taylor, and Deputy Jeffrey Neal** for their devoted friendship. We remain close friends, even today. I would be remiss if I failed to mention the genuine friendship, respect, and pride I shared with many other outstanding coworkers.

Training and teaching others helped me to learn and develop professionally as a law enforcement officer. Also, graduating from the FBI National Academy, Session 187, Quantico, Virginia, was a dream come true to boost my career.

I served my last two academy years as the assistant director of law enforcement training. Before being assigned to the training division, I worked as a traffic crash investigator. Fortunately, I advanced two ranks while assigned to the Academy. I was a happy staffer when the new academy opened in September 1995. I was there to see the concrete poured for the building foundation. We were anxious to deliver quality training consistent with the latest trends, case law, and best practices.

My first SCSO assignment began in the patrol division, rotating shifts while completing nine months of probationary training. I passed probation to earn assignments in urban districts for three years. Smartly, I chose not to become angered by a few misguided deputies with racial jokes and horseplay at the old Sheriff's Substation. I was immune to the bulls—t and refused to be intimidated. I ignored foolishness or nonsense that could easily lead to employee personality conflicts.

I discovered that my presence on the shift threatened several Patrol Division deputies. They underhandedly tried to disparage my work performance. They mocked my Memphis Police relationship with Sheriff Gene Barksdale before he became sheriff. The misguided deputies likely assumed I would receive special favors from Sheriff Barksdale due to our professional friendship. I often found my departmental mail opened and read. A trusted White coworker informed me who the culprits were and what was happening to my incoming mail.

At roll calls, I witnessed the Shift Commander, a lieutenant, instruct patrol deputies to use race as a pretext for making vehicle stops. The lieutenant gave specific instructions to stop vehicles occupied by Black people and Mexicans.

I heard him say, *"If you see 4 to 5 male Blacks or Mexicans riding in a car, stop and check them for warrants because one of them got to be wanted."* I never heard the lieutenant remind his officers to secure sufficient probable cause before making the vehicle stop. I could not believe what I heard in the crowded roll call room.

All Patrol Division deputies were scheduled to report for duty on Fridays unless pre-approved for vacation or bonus time off. Each Friday showed on the weekly roll call as an X-day. The Shift Commander intended his crafty instructions to be proactive strategies to prevent thefts and burglaries in new construction areas. The plan quickly evolved into renegade, discriminatory practices to boost patrol statistics.

Citizens eventually perceived the vehicle stops to be selective harassment targeting people of color. The biased instructions approved by the shift lieutenant prompted needless complaints and lawsuits filed by citizens.

In the minds of the patrol officers, their vehicle stops were successful in deterring construction thefts and burglaries. However, the wrongful practice led to traffic citations being dismissed by the Prosecutor before the Judge heard the court cases. The dismissals reflected negatively on the arresting officer's credibility and, perhaps, disfavored the Sheriff's bid for reelection.

Race or ethnicity should never determine a deputy sheriff's or police officer's decision to stop, interview, frisk, search, or effect an arrest. Pretext stops without legitimate probable cause violate an individual's constitutional rights. Many commanders and subordinates are misguided so long they undoubtedly think they are doing the right thing. They eventually get caught up and self-destruct.

In September 2002, the newly elected Sheriff came aboard the Sheriff's Office with management experience and quality leadership. He effectively transformed the administrative and operational functions to meet national accreditation standards. The Sheriff also improved departmental efficiency 100% with productive meetings and sound fiscal practices. During meetings, he reminded employees about accountability, protecting taxpayer dollars, and his **"MBWA Degree"** *(Management By Walking Around)*. He proudly displayed the MBWA carved letters on his office desk as a novelty piece.

The Sheriff added four Memphis Police retirees to his executive command staff – one Assistant Chief and two Chief Inspectors. He hired the fourth retiree to fill the Chief Deputy's position. Later, the Chief Deputy became the duly elected Sheriff of Shelby County. Two retirees became my supervisors in their respective divisions.

In October 2006, I transferred from the Training Academy to command the Courts & Civil Division, following a promotion to captain in December 2004. I adjusted to the assignment with no apparent problem or reason to believe I would not do an excellent job.

In early 2009, an alarming incident occurred involving the Civil Division personnel and my supervisor. I had decided it would be wise to invite my supervisor to review the Domestic Violence policy with the office clerks and field personnel.

Several deputies in other divisions were facing harsh disciplinary action due to assault allegations reported by their wives and girlfriends. Domestic violence allegations or charges posed severe job consequences for law enforcement, corrections, and civilian personnel.

As Captain, I wanted to be proactive by reminding the supervisors, office clerks, and field personnel to avoid embarrassing personal situations that could jeopardize their jobs. I felt this was an excellent opportunity for my supervisor and me to show we were concerned about our employees.

About 35 employees, primarily Black, assembled in the squad room and greeted my supervisor when he arrived. While addressing the group, he lightly covered the major topics in the Domestic Violence policy before commenting about the mayor and city of Memphis.

At the time, a Black man was serving as Mayor of Memphis. It appeared my supervisor was personally perturbed about some political happenings in Memphis. He disparagingly referred to the mayor as *"King Willie"* and Memphis as *"Willie World."* *"Willie"* happened to be the mayor's first name.

It struck me that my supervisor was a Memphis Police retiree, possibly frustrated over something he had read or heard. His disparaging remarks about the mayor were disrespectful to our employees who resided in the city of Memphis and respected him.

While scanning the room, I saw several Black employees frowning as my supervisor was speaking. When he departed the premises, I sensed someone would complain to me about what he said. However, I wished no one had complained, and his comments would pass over. Consequently, that was not the case.

Sure enough, I received a phone call from a Black female sergeant. She complained that she and other Blacks were offended by my supervisor's comments about the mayor. I assured her I would call and ask my supervisor to return at his convenience and clarify his remarks to avoid further resentment from any employees.

When I called him, I respectfully explained my purpose and asked if he would return to clarify his comments about the mayor and city of Memphis. He reluctantly agreed and returned the next day.

While speaking the second time, I noticed my supervisor did not accept any responsibility for his comments the day before. In other words, to me, he *"tap danced"* around the issue and flaunted his command prerogative to speak as he pleased.

His attitude of indifference shown while clarifying comments appeared out of character for an executive commander. I certainly believed he unconsciously felt no remorse for the disparaging remarks about the mayor and city. In his mind, what he said was right and should be of no consequence to anybody, particularly the Black employees.

When my supervisor asked if his clarification was okay, I said, *"Yes, sir."* I respectfully answered in that manner to avoid appearing insubordinate. Previously, I had sensed that my supervisor was sensitive to my responses. Since he had characterized my responses as *"grandstanding"* following a planning meeting with several subordinates. We were meeting with him at the Homeland Security Emergency Operations Center about court security concerns involving Facility Deputies at the Criminal Justice Complex. The Facility Deputies were under my Homeland Security command.

As time passed, I noticed my supervisor displayed an autocratic *"plantation boss"* mentality, insensitive to any of my suggestions involving operational matters. When we met, I sat and listened because he did most of the talking. In my opinion, his self-righteous opinions and command decisions were often reflective of his political ideology and misguided beliefs. He often displayed a boastful know-it-all attitude with unrelated, overbearing stories about *"guns, hunting, and killing deer."* I respected his rank and position; I was not interested in the ranting stories.

My Captain's rank, decisions, or opinions never appeared to be of any significance to my supervisor. He frequently appeared threatened by my willingness to respectfully speak out candidly on issues.

SIX

Then and Now

Historically, "The origin of *American Policing* can be traced to before and after the Civil War, for purposes of controlling slaves and protecting the interests of slave owners. The use of early slave patrols was one of the precursors of formal police forces in the South" (Turner et al., 2006).

After the Civil War, Southern police departments often carried over aspects of the slave patrols. These included systematic surveillance, the enforcement of curfews, and even notions of who could become a police officer. Though a small number of African Americans joined the police force in the South during Reconstruction, they met active resistance. Though law enforcement looks different today, the profession developed from practices implemented in the colonies (Hansen, 2019).

Police officers must honor their oath of office, duties, and responsibilities with integrity always, enforcing the rule of law with equal justice under the law for all. In my opinion, *"Respect for Law and Order"* is not about respecting a police officer's skin color but what their uniform represents.

I argue that *American Policing* must uphold the fundamental principles and values it represents, unbound from the systemic racial hypocrisy that cripples it. I dispel the false, broad-brush assumption that *"most Black people are likely to be thugs or criminals."* Inaccurate beliefs and perceptions have invariably misguided too many White police officers.

Through the years, Truth, Transparency, and Accountability hardly ever mattered for White police officers. They often avoided prosecution for their misconduct by deceit or design, especially in the South. News reports abroad show that White officers disproportionately violated Black citizens' civil rights and liberties without any consequence.

For the most part, laws, policies, and practices are now changing for the better. A growing number of police departments have begun to pick up their broken pieces and initiate meaningful reform with substantive solutions. Writing *Misguided Badges* and telling the truth to help bridge the racial divide has set me free.

According to a Wall Street Journal article, the New York Police (NYPD) and 70 departments have enrolled in a collaborative reform program to teach officers to intervene when another officer uses excessive force or violates department guidelines. Georgetown University Law Center reportedly launched the program in June 2020. The article, "NYPD Officers to Get Training on Speaking Up Against Bad

Policing," by Alan Neuhauser, was published on January 28, 2021.

The Tennessee Governor's Office featured another reform model for law enforcement agencies across the state. Governor Bill Lee announced the Law Enforcement Reform Partnership on July 2, 2020. Governor Lee said, "I am confident the outcomes of this partnership will help ensure our law enforcement officials are efficiently protecting communities across the state while serving every Tennessean with dignity and respect."

The collaborative initiative provides critical enhancements for strengthening police accountability, improving information-sharing, and increasing officer training. Hats off to the state of Tennessee for moving in the right direction.

Widespread protests and police-involved killings of unarmed Black victims have provoked a new public distrust against police officers. The evidential details captured by video cameras have overwhelmingly justified misconduct allegations against misguided police officers. Attorneys general and civil rights lawyers are successfully prosecuting misguided officers and influencing policing practices across the country. Today, more police officers are facing prosecution than ever before.

Body-worn and cellphone cameras continue to provide indisputable evidence confirming the disproportionate use of unreasonable, excessive force against Black citizens. The lack of transparency and refusal to prosecute or convict misguided police officers have derailed public trust in Black communities.

Ironically, the release of video camera evidence has exposed misconduct allegations to benefit both police officers and citizens. Nationwide protests and incidents of excessive force have sparked a national outcry to *"Defund"* and *"Reform"* police departments to restore public trust. Thank GOD for body-worn cameras and personal cellphones; enough is enough. I predict that correcting misguided police officers and eradicating systemic racism -- in America -- will be an enormous challenge for years to come.

My firsthand experiences raise awareness that national calls for police reform are justifiable and overdue. However, emotional demands to *"Defund"* police department budgets at the expense of public safety are not sound solutions. I serve notice that crime rates are steadily increasing, not decreasing.

Police-involved shootings and killings of unarmed Black victims continually create a racial divide beyond denial. Concerned police officials, politicians, and citizens scramble for common ground to bridge the divide with workable solutions. I suggest that admitting the truth, supporting meaningful reform, facilitating diversity training, and holding police officers accountable would be a good start. During many of the shootings or fatal incidents, police officers ignored de-escalation options to avoid deadly force.

Nowadays, police and sheriff departments continue to pay costly legal settlements because of permissive supervisors, rebellious subordinates, and discriminatory practices. Too often, permissive supervisors consciously turn a blind eye allowing misguided officers to violate standards of ethical conduct without consequence. When police supervisors allow misconduct or destructive behavior to go unchecked, they, too, must be held accountable.

It would certainly help calm racial tension and improve public trust if police officials and partisan politicians accepted responsibility for apparent mistakes or failures. Truth, Transparency, and Accountability are essential elements for sustaining public trust.

****

Meanwhile, I was at peace with the *"Good-cop"* conscience and policing philosophy I embraced as a young police officer. I contributed my best to be the best. The behavior of violators or offenders dictated my decisions and outcomes on occasions. I did what was necessary to maintain safety and control of any given situation. Mistreating or physically abusing people did not represent my work personality by any means.

Please do not admonish me for being unashamed to admit the truth. You see, if I did not accept the facts, my moral conscience would not allow me to live with myself. I characterize the obnoxious attitudes and behavior I witnessed from so-called police professionals as the epitome of absurdity. GOD knows; I reached out many times beyond the call of duty to help others. I challenge other police officers and citizens to search their souls and do the same.

Denial, harboring hate, and projecting blame must not be options for escaping the truth about *American Policing* and its influence on systemic racism. I contend that *American Policing* evolved to be problematic for Black citizens and police officers alike.

The following story, **"Yes, Black America Fears the Police. Here's Why,"** was written by ProPublica's Nikole Hannah-Jones and co-published with Politico Magazine. ProPublica is a nonprofit newsroom that investigates abuses of power.

I view the teachable excerpts from the story insightful as shared on one hand and deeply problematic on the other hand. Most Black citizens and the American policing culture are yet light years apart. Trust, respect, and understanding are crucial to establishing positive relationships.

We are not criminals because we are Black. Nor are we somehow the only people in America who don't want to live in safe neighborhoods. Yet many of us cannot fundamentally trust the people who are charged with keeping us and our communities safe (Hannah-Jones, 2015).

For Black Americans, policing is "the most enduring aspect of the struggle for civil rights," says Muhammad, a historian, and director of the Schomburg Center for Research in Black Culture in New York. "It has always been the mechanism for racial surveillance and control" (Hannah-Jones, 2015).

In the South, police once did the dirty work of enforcing the racial caste system. The Ku Klux Klan and law enforcement were often indistinguishable. Black-and-white photographs of the era memorialize the way Southern police sicced German shepherds on civil rights protesters and peeled the skin off Black children with the force of water hoses. Lawmen were also involved or implicated in untold numbers of beatings, killings, and disappearances of Black Southerners who forgot their place (Hannah-Jones, 2015).

In the North, police worked to protect White spaces by containing and controlling the rising Black population that propelled into the industrial belt during the Great Migration. It was not unusual for Northern police to join White mobs as they attacked Black homeowners attempting to move into White neighborhoods, or Black workers trying to take jobs reserved for White laborers. They strictly enforced vagrancy offenses and other common laws that gave broad discretion to stop, question, and arrest Black citizens at will (Hannah-Jones, 2015).

Much has changed since then. Much has not (Hannah-Jones, 2015).

Young Black men today are 21-times more likely to be shot and killed by police than young White men. Still, it's not that Black Americans expect to die every time they encounter the police. Police killings are just the worst manifestations of countless slights and indignities that build until there's an explosion (Hannah-Jones, 2015).

Black communities want a good relationship with law enforcement because they want their families and property to be safe. After all, it is true that Black communities often face higher rates of crime; in 2013, more than 50 percent of murder victims across the country were Black, though only 13 percent of the total population is. But it's also true that crime reduction efforts by Black people in Black communities have contributed to the recent, historic drop in crime across the country (Hannah-Jones, 2015).

So why are Black Americans still so often denied the same kind of smart policing that typically occurs in White communities, where police seem fully capable of discerning between law-abiding citizens and those committing crimes, and between crimes like turnstile-jumping and those that need serious intervention (Hannah-Jones, 2015)?

"You can be protected and served," Muhammad says. "It happens every day in communities across America. It happens all the time in white communities where crime is happening" (Hannah-Jones, 2015).

I agree that police presence is necessary to maintain law and order in any Black, brown, or white community. Also, I agree that most Black citizens resent the aggressive, renegade policing tactics deployed in their communities. I am certainly not inferring that all White police officers are racist cops mistreating Black citizens. Common sense compels me to urge Black citizens to share responsibility and cooperate with honorable police officers to clean up crimes that devastate underserved communities.

In Black urban communities, *"Gun Violence"* is notably an increased threat to public safety and quality of life. Daily news reports indicate that a record number of adults and innocent children are shot and killed by this nonsense. How long must parents, relatives, and neighbors live with this torment? This madness must stop.

Maltreatment by police officers, incendiary rhetoric spewed by politicians, and violent protests by citizens certainly do not help matters. Police, politicians, and community leaders must collaborate responsibly to find thoughtful solutions for effective change.

District Attorneys should prosecute guilty suspects for violent crimes in Black communities to the full extent of the law. Nevertheless, the same applies to any community. In a civil society, we must respect law enforcement and support the men and women who nobly serve as police officers. "Law & Order" is not an option; it is a dire necessity in every sense of the word.

Today, racial tension between police officers and Black citizens is at a fever pitch. "Misguided Badges" exposes the "Us vs. Them" mentality that continually derails public trust. Building trust and establishing positive relationships are crucial to any police department's mission. Let us pray that police officials will be forthright and accountable while improving our policing culture with best practices.

The purpose of law enforcement in a free society is to sustain public safety and uphold the rule of law for continuing peace and liberty. Trust and accountability between police officers and citizens are paramount. The government holds the power to exercise force in achieving its ends but must protect the rights of all community members. Best practices require that police officers build relationships within their communities, respect civil liberties, and avoid tactics that encourage the use of excessive force against citizens (Charles Koch Institute, n.d.).

I harbored no ill-will or bitterness while writing this Memoir. My on-the-job challenges and firsthand experiences distinctively contrasted those of White officers. Despite occasional anguish, I was undeterred by nonsense, opened to change, and smartly focused on learning my job.

SEVEN

What Is It Like to be a Black Police Officer?

Surviving offensive experiences helped me to maintain self-control and safeguard my credibility relative to who I am. You see, as a Black police officer, the only thing I owned was my credibility. If I lost, sold, or allowed someone to rob me of my credibility, then I ceased to be a man or who I am. Doing neither was indicative of my nature, even under uncontrollable circumstances.

Through the years, too often, systemic racism robbed Black police officers of advancement opportunities because of skin color. Historical facts and lived experiences broadly support my contention. I am willing to wager that this Memoir speaks to similar experiences and injustices lived by other Black officers across the country. "Misguided Badges" provide readers with some gut-wrenching perspectives of shared experiences by Black officers and citizens.

Black police officers in Memphis struggled to secure legitimacy in search of respect in a resentful work environment. In demanding respect, there were times when tempers flared, and Black egos overshadowed common sense. However, police employment offered a secure and stable job with good benefits. Black police officers hung in there – through adversity and abuse -- and turned negatives into positives.

As a rookie, several White officers often told me, *"Yarbrough, you are alright."* When they realized I heard them disparaging Black defendants with racial slurs, some remarked, *"We don't mean you."* Those officers were comfortable in arbitrarily taking me for granted. I perceived their phony disclaimer to be unworthy of any afterthought whatsoever.

However, I chose not to dignify nor glorify any of their derogative comments with a subservient response. I smartly reacted with common sense responses. *"Go along to get along"* was not a common brainwash for me to swallow or follow.

The Washington Times spoke with a half-dozen active or retired Black officers about their experiences. They all said they had experienced racism on the job, including White officers' refusals to speak with them and finding a noose hanging in their squad car. *"We don't speak up because it's career suicide,"* said <u>Regina Coward</u>, who recently retired after 27 years with the Las Vegas Metropolitan Police Department. "We let a lot of things slide because we know for a fact that when we speak up, we get locked out. So, we just go along with the program because there is no consequence" (Mordock, 2020).

The "Go along to Get along" mentality led to undue stress and a depressive state of mind for many Black police officers. This mentality affected those who were satisfied or afraid of change's consequences, oblivious to making things better for themselves or others. Some found themselves adapting and contributing to the same problematic culture that resented their presence.

It is apparent Black police officers did what they had to do to keep their jobs and feed their families. Their mental grit, tenacity, and sacrifice proved to be good examples for me and others to follow.

On the contrary, I knew Black officers who refused to endure the racist policing culture in Memphis during the 1960s and throughout the 20th century. They moved on to other job professions abroad only to experience similar racist conditions. Nevertheless, systemic racism and racial injustices were inescapable for Blacks all over the country.

Meanwhile, I survived a respectable law enforcement career spanning 46 years, committed to honoring equal justice under the law for all. I adopted an open-minded policing philosophy that challenged me to *"Do the right thing and treat others as I would want them to treat me."* That, I did do. However, on occasions, I was subjected to *"See and Don't See"* and *"Hear and Don't Hear."*

I prayed to GOD for divine guidance to avoid corruption by defiant coworkers. I focused on my *"Granddaddy & Lil Mama's"* conventional wisdom: *The truth shall set you free.* I cannot and will not ever disavow the life values my parents instilled in me. For this reason, fear was not an option whatsoever. **Ms. Rosa Parks, a civil rights trailblazer, once said, *"You must never be fearful about what you are doing when it is right."***

Occasionally, disgruntled White partners chose not to talk to me unless it was a dire necessity. Once they were comfortable that I was trustworthy and not a *"snitch,"* I was regarded as a *"good ole boy."* Meaning my partners felt free to say and do whatever without me becoming upset.

One day, while joking with each other, a White partner said to me, *"You know, Yarbrough, you're a good ole Nigger."* I responded, *"Yea, and you're a good ole Cracker, too."* We both laughed heartily. Hearing racial slurs was just a harsh reality Black officers endured during the 1960s, 70s, 80s, and now. Regardless, I was determined to stay on the job – and I did.

Black officers were vulnerable to hostile workplaces that resisted change. Several times, while awaiting roll call, I overheard jokes about making *"the Coons"* quit. Did it get on my nerves? Yes, it did. But I ignored it and moved on. I controlled myself, aware of the *"deck of cards"* I was dealing with each day. I can honestly say the veteran partners who trained me knew their job very well.

My regular partners and I developed a bond; we respected and understood each other. My life depended on their life; their life depended on my life. Regardless, mistreating or hating someone because of their race, gender, or skin color was not in my nature. I bonded with a keen sense of loyalty and sometimes became defensive about racial allegations others lodged against my partners.

Some Black officers became partners to corruption, knowing what they were doing was wrong. It took courage for them to defy the wrongdoing and convince White partners to do the right thing. No one can make a police officer do wrong or mistreat anybody; they commit misconduct by choice. No police officer should ever defend or condone another officer's wrongdoing to persecute another human being. I believe the following is true for any law enforcement agency.

On any given day, in any police department in the nation, 15 percent of officers will do the right thing no matter what is happening. Fifteen percent of officers will abuse their authority at every opportunity. The remaining 70 percent could go either way, depending on whom they are working with (Hudson, 2016).

Likely, the coming of Black police officers in Memphis led Black civil rights activists to berate and label the officers as *"window dressing"* or *"tokens."* Black activists felt that Black officers portrayed a subservient role, complicit with White officers' thoughts and social standards. They falsely alleged that Black officers emulated the abusive behavior of White officers for acceptance.

In many cases, Black police officers adapted to the *"Go Along to Get Along"* mindset to protect their jobs. They survived between *"a rock and a hard place."* The officers had no choice but to do what they had to do, *"catching hell"* and enduring continuous abuse from White officers. During their era, Malcolm X and James Baldwin might have labeled most Black officers as *"Field Niggers"* or *"House Niggers."*

In other professions, too, some Blacks were better at playing the *"token role"* than others. Law Enforcement was no different for Blacks than any other profession. In contrast, sworn police officers were granted the constitutional right to physically arrest individuals who violated the rule of law.

However, Black officers in Memphis could not physically arrest White people until around 1963. Black officers could only detain White people. They called for White officers to search and effect a physical arrest if deemed necessary. This hypocrisy was a sign of the segregated times in the South.

The first Black officers hired in Memphis only policed Black people in the Beale Street area. I learned that White supervisors bragged for the Black officers to fail their walking patrol assignments. Several supervisors were heard saying, *"When a couple of those Niggers get their asses whipped good most of them will quit."* However, the intimidation tactics and mind games failed. Black officers continually overcame combative confrontations on and around Beale

Street. I am grateful for their trailblazing courage and survival.

I was told the old Beale Street stayed crowded exclusively with Black people, featuring Black entertainers and "Barrel House Blues." Beale Street gained worldwide notoriety as the *"Home of the Blues,"* with W.C. Handy, B.B. King, Rufus Thomas, Little Milton, and Bobby Blue Bland. Today, the crowds and entertainment dynamics are quite different. Beale Street attracts tourists of all races and ethnic groups from all over the world.

In other U.S. cities, Black officers were motivated by similar experiences to become police officers. In June 2020, the following National Public Radio (NPR) interviews provided three generations of actuality to support shared similarities. Three perspectives covered: *"What it Is like to be a Black police officer."*

National Public Radio's Ari Shapiro speaks with Isaiah McKinnon, Cheryl Dorsey, and Vincent Montague, three police officers of different generations, about Black's experiences in law enforcement.

AILSA CHANG, HOST:
Today and tomorrow, we're going to explore what the national debate over race and policing looks like from the inside, inside the police force, and inside the

African American community. Here's our co-host Ari Shapiro.

ARI SHAPIRO, BYLINE: We invited three generations of Black police officers to join us for a wide-ranging conversation about what's changed over the decades, what hasn't, and what they make of this moment in America.

ISAIAH MCKINNON: It should be recording. There we go.

SHAPIRO: First, meet Isaiah McKinnon. He's in his 70s, retired. He served as chief of police and deputy mayor in the city of Detroit. He joined the force in the 1960s.

MCKINNON: These guys would do things to you to force people to quit.

SHAPIRO: Next, Cheryl Dorsey. She joined the Los Angeles Police Department in 1980. She's also retired now after a long career with the LAPD.

CHERYL DORSEY: I'm a Black woman first, and I am a mother of four Black men second. And then third, I happen to be a sergeant of police.

SHAPIRO: Finally, Vincent Montague is 37 and president of the Black Shield Police Association, supporting officers serving in the Greater Cleveland area. He's been in law enforcement for 12 years.

VINCENT MONTAGUE: When I'm at work, it's almost as if you're a chameleon. You must adapt to the culture of the job.

SHAPIRO: I started by asking the three of them why they wanted to get into police work.

DORSEY: Chief, why don't you go first?

MCKINNON: I decided to become a police officer due to a severe beating I received in 1957 as a young boy by a group in Detroit called the Big Four. They were usually four large white officers. I was leaving school, and these four officers grabbed me, threw me up against a car, and proceeded to beat me brutally, and then at some point told me to get my a** out of there, and I ran home. So, I decided that evening I was going to become a police officer. Certainly, I didn't know I was going to become chief. But that was the impetus for me becoming a police officer in 1957. I joined the Detroit Police Department in 1965.

SHAPIRO: I was thinking about the kind of person who has an experience like that and decides that I'm going to go in that direction instead of running away from that. I'm going to become a police officer and try to make a change from the inside. And I thought what that says about the kind of person you are.

MCKINNON: Well, it was so important for me because I had seen these officers beat up so many people in my neighborhood. We had - I think that Detroit had 5,500 police officers at the time, and probably less than 50 were African American. And it was important for me to try and do something from within.

SHAPIRO: Cheryl, what was your path? And going in, did you have hesitations about joining a police force with a reputation of hostility towards Black people?

DORSEY: No. I was very selfish because I was selfishly motivated. I was a young mother. I had been married and was going through a divorce. I had a small child, and I had bills. And it was strictly a financial decision. I had many friends who didn't want to be friends with me anymore when they realized what I was thinking about doing. I had family members who had interactions with the police. I remember seeing things. Although I grew up very middle class, I never had any negative interactions with the police. But it was strictly, I need money, and who can get it to me.

SHAPIRO: Vincent, tell us your story.

MONTAGUE: The school that I went to growing up, I was typically the minority there. So, the neighborhood I grew up in was separated from - like, Garfield was the suburb, and Cleveland was the city. So, where I live, I was one of the students who divided the neighborhood up that we had to go to Garfield schools. So, Garfield schools are predominantly white. And this was in the early '90s. I was playing a kickball game with some students, and they were White kids. And I gave him a high five, and this white kid just started stabbing me in the back with a pencil.

SHAPIRO: Literally stabbing you in the back?

MONTAGUE: Yes. He thought that I was attacking the White males that we were playing a kickball game with. But that was my first experience with racism. That kind of led me to become a police officer because

I wanted to make changes in the community that I lived in.

SHAPIRO: So, for all three of you, did you experience tension between your identity in uniform and out of uniform, going from the police force back to your community every day?

MCKINNON: My first night as a Detroit police officer and the supervisors, the sergeant, and lieutenant came into the room, and they announced roll call. And as they announced the assignments, they announced this one officer's name, and they gave the assignment. Then they said, McKinnon, scout 27. And this officer said Jesus' effing Christ. I'm working with the - and he said the racially derogatory term.

SHAPIRO: The N-word?

MCKINNON: This was my welcome to the Detroit Police Department. Yes. Yeah. And so, I rode with him for eight hours, and he never said a word to me. And it's just interesting because when I went out to the street, the Black people didn't talk to me either because I was a turncoat. So, it was a difficult time.

SHAPIRO: So, Cheryl and Vincent, how much of what Isaiah is saying sounds familiar to you, and how much was different when you became a police officer?

DORSEY: Well, you know, I joined 20 years later, and everything he's talking about was still going on. And my experiences were pretty much similar. I had to turtle up. I had to get a hard shell. I had a training officer who put me on a pain compliance hold. It's called a twist lock. Like we were taught and trained to do suspects when you're trying to handcuff them, this is what my training officer is doing to me with about three, four months in the field. There were several officers in the room, and they're just sitting looking. But one of them was a Black officer who had a little time on the job, and he had a little size to him. And he said, hey, hey, stop that. And he made him let me go.

SHAPIRO: Wow. So more than 20 years later, Vincent, you join the police force. And how similar is your experience to what you've heard from Cheryl and Isaiah?

MONTAGUE: Well, I joined the police force in 2008. I think things were - are more covert on how things were handled. In the police academy, you find out who people were in that police academy. I would say the Academy was very divided. They tried to bring us together, but frequently Black officers were told you must have thick skin to deal with this because if you can't handle what they're saying in the Academy, you can't take it on the streets. So that's what we were told. But it was different for officers that didn't look like us. They were not told those same things.

DORSEY: You know, it's interesting, if I can say this, Ari, that you have - you know, we're almost three generations, right? You've got the '60s, the '80s, and the 2000s, and all our experiences are the same. And folks ask me, you know, well, why would you want anyone to do this going forward? Because if we're not on these police departments, you know, we can't have an impact. While I'm troubled by what I'm hearing, each of us has gone through this, and you would think that the chief's experiences would have made it better for me and mine for Vincent, not so much. And so that part saddens me.

SHAPIRO: And we'll hear more tomorrow from Cheryl Dorsey, Isaiah McKinnon, and Vincent Montague about this moment in America (National Public Radio [NPR], 2020).

EIGHT

New Truth vs. Old Truth

Today, the American policing culture is broken throughout the country. The disproportionate use of deadly force against Black citizens by misguided police officers is overwhelming. This phenomenon has tarnished American policing since the post-Civil War era. A *"New Truth"* of meaningful police reforms must replace an *"Old Truth"* of systemic racism. It is time for healing and accepting responsibility for transforming the broken culture for the better. We owe it to the next generation.

Everybody loses when police and citizens fail to work together responsibly with common goals and objectives. Today, mutual trust is essential to sustaining positive relationships between the police and Black citizens.

Police officers, everywhere, are the face of the communities they protect and serve. They are public servants held to a higher standard, consummated with integrity, courage, and loyalty. Police officers are sworn to an oath of office to perform duties governed by the rule of law and standards of conduct. They are human beings, too, likely to experience the same personal problems as any law-abiding civilian.

As peacekeepers — not warriors— police officers must harness their energy to be part of a solution, not a problem. Misguided police officers remain shortsighted with false assumptions that Black people possess negative life values while White people possess positive ones. I find this biased, self-righteous mindset to be problematic. It has carried over to negatively influence policing duties, responsibilities, and practices. Persecuting people because of their nationality, race, color, religion, or political persuasion is morally wrong and has no place in law enforcement, period.

Over the years, misguided police officers consistently disregarded laws and policies, violating the inalienable rights, freedoms, and liberties of Black people. As a result, innocent Black people have been unjustifiably incarcerated and put to death.

Nevertheless, Black citizens must respect law and order and understand that all White police officers are not racist bigots or bad apples. Conversely, White police officers must not arbitrarily label Black citizens as inferior because of their skin color. All people have a right to equal justice under the law regardless of race or ethnicity.

Moreover, I believe that police reforms are inevitable during these times of distrust. Also, I reject the commonly spoken insult that all Black police officers are *"Sell-outs"* or *"Uncle Toms."* In contrast, I denounce the insult that all White police officers are racist. Neither is right by any stretch of one's imagination.

According to a PEW Research Center survey in 2016, the following data may account for some White police officers' misguidance.

On the broader question of overall race relations in American society, the overwhelming majority (92%) of White officers say the U.S. has made the changes needed to give blacks equal rights with whites; just 29% of Black officers agree. The public is divided along racial lines on this question, too, but not as much as police officers: About six-in-ten whites (57%) say the country has made the changes needed to bring about equal rights for blacks, compared with just 12% of blacks (Gramlich, 2017).

I subscribed to the common-sense theory that changing a racist policing culture requires changing officers' attitudes and behavior. I am reminded of an old truism, *"A flat tire will not go anywhere until you change it."* When unlawful police actions go unnoticed and unaddressed, they become accepted behavior. Subsequently, lawsuit settlements are likely beneficial to plaintiffs and costly ($$$) to taxpayers.

African Americans have long protested and endured a racist policing culture since the 1870s and throughout the 20th century. News archives of violent uprisings in major U.S.

cities can verify this as a fact (Corbould, 2020).

Widespread protests have drawn attention to recent police-involved deaths, prompting an urgent call for reforms to transform a problematic policing culture. Public demonstrations have long been a productive way to gain attention and bring about effective change.

I contend that public safety and quality of life suffer when police department budgets are cut or defunded. Less funding for essential police services will cause a reduction in the delivery of services and an increase in crime rates, severely affecting underserved communities. In some small towns, police officers may be combating crime and lawlessness with limited budget funds.

I suggest that well-thought-out plans be studied to improve mental health training for police departments. Perhaps mental health providers could assist police officers with nonviolent mental health calls. Mental health training is too limited for police departments to guarantee consumers an effective response and safe outcome.

Simply arresting and transporting mental health consumers to jail is not always the appropriate response or solution. However, safety is still paramount for any response. Cutting police budgets is likely to diminish police responsibilities. Maintaining the same service capacity with insufficient funding creates substantial risks for any police department.

I contend that *"defunding"* police departments is a no-no

without careful thought. In a survey about public attitudes toward law enforcement, two-thirds of respondents said that individual officers should be held legally accountable for using excessive force. Few of those polled said they would support cutting police budgets (Neuman, 2020).

NINE

Speaking Truth to Power

Speaking Truth to Power: LEARNING about other people is relevant to UNDERSTANDING other people. LEARNING to UNDERSTAND other people is crucial for racial healing, building trust, and establishing positive relationships.

Based on news accounts and personal experiences, I am persuaded that the American policing culture was — and still is — a broken cornerstone of systemic racism that defaces our democracy. American democracy never afforded Black citizens equitable social justice as compared to White citizens. As a result, abhorrent practices and racial injustices remain common to all phases of our criminal justice system: Law Enforcement, Courts, and Corrections. Overwhelmingly, telling the TRUTH matters given the nationwide tension created by negative relationships, events, and outcomes involving Black citizens and police officers.

Over the years, I discovered that most White officers avoided conversations about Black history and race relations. I asked myself repeatedly, *"Why are they afraid?"* Some withdrew and displayed a short-fused disposition as if they were de facto experts on Black people. Maybe, discussing history and race relations was a no-no because of their inherent bias, guilt, or miseducation about Black people.

In many instances, White officers perceived Black people as lawbreakers and inferior human beings. I attributed their biased misperceptions to the *"Us vs. Them"* policing mindset, warped values, and a refusal to accept change. Perhaps, if those misguided officers better understood what they misperceived about Black people, their attitudes and behavior might differ. I found most of their thoughts and perceptions regarding critical racial issues to be ridiculous – the epitome of ignorance.

A state lawmaker who represents Chicago's West Side introduced legislation that would require all police officers in Illinois to be schooled on the intersection of law, race, and racism in the hopes of teaching officers *"the culture and the lifestyles of different communities and people" (Hinton, 2021).*

"If we want to change the behavior of police, we have to educate them," state Rep. La Shawn Ford said.

The West Side Democrat said requiring officers to learn critical race theory is about *"tackling racism"* and *"becoming aware of our very own shortcomings and ignorance about our peers."*

But the head of the Chicago union for rank-and-file police officers said the bill is *"redundant and ridiculous."*

"They're going to get officers killed with this constant nonsense of 'race, race, race,'" said John Catanzara Jr., the president of the Chicago Fraternal Order of Police. *"You're gonna have people so paranoid to do their job they're going to be worried about race more than they're worried about reacting to a threat."*

The legislation would amend the state's police training law and create a *"critical race theory academy"* comprised of members ranging from scholars to sociologists and community organizers who are experts in the theory and members of the General Assembly and law enforcement officers (Hinton, 2021).

I am an ardent believer in community policing, critical race theory, and meaningful police reforms. They are easy decisions for me. I concur wholeheartedly with state Representative LaShawn Ford (D-IL). Police officers should be taught how racism, 'ignorance' prevent them from impartially doing their job (Hinton, 2021).

I talked to both White and Black officers who opposed police reform and any mention of Critical Race Theory (CRT). Unbelievably, some even remained narrow-minded in their second thoughts about the importance of community policing. Notably, the White officers felt that reforms were a waste of time and resources, and CRT was propaganda manipulated by political left-wingers. Most were steadfast in saying, *"Move out of the way and let the police officers do their job."*

QUESTION: What is Critical Race Theory (CRT)? I certainly view it as not being *"political propaganda"* as declared by outspoken misguided police officers and right-wing politicians.

Dr. Joseph H. Silver, Sr.

Dr. Joseph H. Silver, Sr., President of Silver & Associates, a full-service education consulting firm based in Atlanta and Savannah, Georgia, provides enlightening perspectives below on Critical Race Theory. On June 30, 2021, his perspectives were published by the Savannah Tribune in an article entitled, *"Critical Race Theory--What Is All the Fuss About?"*

Dr. Silver, a native of North Carolina, is highly recognized regionally, nationally, and internationally as a transformational and innovative leader, educator, and consultant in the global education market. He has served as President of Alabama State University, Provost and Vice President of Academic Affairs at Clark Atlanta University, Vice President and Professor of Political Science at Savannah State University, Administrative Fellow with the Board of Regents of the University Systems of Georgia, and Associate Professor of Political Science and Assistant to the President of Kennesaw State College. In addition, Dr. Silver has acquired a host of leadership awards and innovative accomplishments to his credit.

Critical Race Theory has been around since the 1970s. However, the concept has gained interest among those who seek to rewrite history and silence the voices of those who seek to make sure that the realities of history are known, no matter how bad they are. Critical race theory is a framework to better understand historical, social, political, and economic phenomena. Critical race theory seeks to explain racism from a structural and institutional context. While race plays a critical role in every aspect of our lives, critical race theorists argue that race is not a natural concept. Rather, it is a man-made social construct to maintain a superior and dominant position for white people.

One of the basic tenets of critical race theory is that while all White folk are not racist, they benefit from a fundamentally structured system to maintain white supremacy and white privilege. So, otherwise good white folk remain silent or choose to ignore the maltreatment of Blacks so as not to interrupt their white privileges. Therefore, race plays a role in the criminal justice and legal systems as well as the economic and political systems. Politicians are now saying that racism does not exist in the state or the country. The sad but true part of this assertion is that because White people have not experienced racism, it is difficult to grasp the reality of racism. However, Black people experience racism daily because it is a "lived reality" in the circles of their lives.

Because white people have historically controlled the education system, they have determined the curriculum. They determine what is taught and how things are taught. As a result, many of the tragedies that Black people experienced were not and are not disclosed in the curriculum or taught in the classrooms in schools across this county. When these tragedies are disclosed, it has been done in a filtered manner that either made Black folk the villains or in a manner that suggested they were "getting what they deserved (Savannah Tribune, 2021).

Dr. Silver continued with a striking, thought-provoking statement for readers to consider. He asserted, *"After all, America tells the rest of the world about the beauty of democracy. Doesn't it seem a bit hypocritical for those in power to be suppressing the truth, the vote, and free-thinking?"*

Dr. Silver spoke *"Truth to Power"* that should weigh heavily on the minds of all Americans. He realistically exposed a moral decay that continually tarnishes our democracy. His simplified perspective on critical race theory is outstanding. I was intrigued by his points of view. They enhanced my sense of understanding tremendously about critical race theory.

I personally view *"Critical Race Theory"* as an eye-opener that serves the educational purpose of teaching untold history linking slavery, race, and systemic racism. Comparative analyses of systemic racism and injustices – *then and now* – are examined for racial understanding and healing. Critical race theory raises awareness, provokes critical thinking, enhances learning, and eradicates miseducation.

Critical race theory sprang up in the mid-1970s, as several lawyers, activists, and legal scholars across the country realized, simultaneously, that the heady advances of the civil rights era of the 1960s had stalled and, in many respects, were being rolled back. Realizing that new theories and strategies were needed to combat the subtler forms of racism gaining ground, early writers such as Derrick Bell, Alan Freeman, and Richard Delgado (coauthor of this primer) put their minds to the task. Others joined them, and the group held its first conference at a convent outside Madison, Wisconsin, in the summer of 1989 (Volpe, 2020).

How did Critical Race Theory (CRT) gain traction? A national reckoning over racial injustices and police brutality began in 2020 in the wake of George Floyd's murder in Minneapolis. The national discussion intensified after the publication of the New York Times' 1619 Project, which reframed the founding of America around slavery (Richards & Wong, 2021).

Republican lawmakers in GOP-controlled states have since pursued legislation that restricts how race and racism can be taught in public schools. At least 28 states have sought to restrict teaching about racism or bias in schools, according to Chalkbeat, a nonprofit education news site (Richards & Wong, 2021).

According to several national news reports, police unions are speaking out to support misguided officers in denouncing critical race theory. Many are disgruntled with comparisons made between modern police behavior and mob killings of blacks in the 19th and 20th centuries (Miles, 2016).

Some police unions and misguided members continue to push distorted political reports and conspiracy theories – at any cost -- to distract from the truth and resist calls for thoughtful police reform.

On June 16, 2021, one such news example started at the Hudson Catholic High School in Jersey City, New Jersey.

Social media criticism erupted over an instructor's assignment to compare lynching with the police killing of Black Americans. The assignment intended to encourage a thoughtful dialogue of post-Civil War and modern-day racism and violence against African Americans. It followed comprehensive classroom presentations and discussions on promoting better communication and information to ensure fair and equal treatment of all people. The instructor and school administration regret any concern or misunderstanding this issue may have caused. The controversial assignment was first reported by NBC (D'Auria, 2021).

The history of police brutality and oppression — against Black people—needs to be taught and shared by our schools. Where can we find better academic sources than schools to learn and understand how American history influenced systemic racism?

Today, history seems to repeat itself. How can our nation avoid shameless hypocrisy if people are limited in knowledge about historical facts? Education must afford all Americans a level playing field to learn and understand.

I know that national news sources can verify reprehensible accounts of past lynching and killing of innocent Black Americans. The below facts and details speak for themselves and must be available to all for equitable research and meaningful dialogue.

Police killings of black people in the United States are reminiscent of lynching. The government must do far more to protect them, a United Nations working group says in a report that will be debated at the U.N. Human Rights Council (Miles, 2016).

The hard-hitting criticism - drawing a comparison between modern police behavior and mob killings of blacks in the 19th and 20th centuries - comes at the height of racial tension in the United States. This "Contemporary police killings and the trauma that they create are reminiscent of the past racial terror of lynching," said the report by the U.N. Working Group of Experts on People of African Descent. Most lynching victims died by hanging (Miles, 2016).

A 2015 report by a non-profit organization, the Equal Justice Initiative, said 3,959 black people were killed in "racial terror lynching" in a dozen southern states between 1877 and 1950. The U.N. expert report was based on a visit to the United States in January by a five-member group chaired by Filipino law professor Ricardo A. Sunga III. Since the visit, anger over police tactics has risen as their fatal encounters with African Americans, many of them unarmed, have sparked protests and unrest across the country (Miles, 2016).

Although the United States has made efforts at reform, the group said it remained "extremely concerned" about the human rights situation of African Americans. "In particular, the legacy of colonial history, enslavement, racial subordination and segregation, racial terrorism, and racial inequality in the United States remains a serious challenge, as there has been no real commitment to reparations and truth and reconciliation for people of African descent. "Impunity for State violence has resulted in the current human rights crisis and must be addressed as a matter of urgency" (Miles, 2016).

Police killings go unpunished because initial investigations are usually conducted by the police department where the alleged perpetrator works because prosecutors have a wide range of discretion over presenting charges. Because the use of force is not subject to international standards, the experts' group said. They recommended the United States create a reliable national system to track killings and excessive use of force by law enforcement officials and end racial profiling, which is "a rampant practice and seriously damages the trust between African Americans and law enforcement officials" (Miles, 2016).

To improve race relations, education should be "accompanied by acts of reconciliation" to overcome bigotry and past injustices, while federal and state laws should recognize the negative impact of enslavement and racial injustice, the report added (Miles, 2016).

If we cannot embrace the truth about American history for a better understanding to remedy the racial pain that torments our nation, we are doomed to repeat it. Because American history – without a doubt – encompasses slavery, segregation, and systemic racism. Those societal ills negatively influenced America's social justice, race relations, and quality of life.

I contend that our nation must PROGRESS in the best interest of racial harmony and decency. Race relations for the better are way overdue. RACIAL BIGOTRY, IGNORANCE, and HYPOCRISY should never represent or define American democracy. The American policing culture must conform to the Constitutional rights and liberties granted to every American citizen, regardless of race, ethnicity, gender, or skin color.

TEN

Conclusion: What is the Answer

I share excerpts from a news article, *"Accountability for Bad Apples: Police Reforms to Restore Faith in Institutions,"* by Jacqueline Varas, published March 22, 2021. The excerpts reinforced my thoughts and beliefs about contemporary law enforcement. The informative article helps to educate police officers, politicians, and citizens with facts and perspectives for healing and understanding.

The widely publicized deaths of Floyd, Taylor and several other Black Americans over the past few years have weakened trust, sparked outrage, and led to widespread demands for increased police accountability across the nation. These also have led to peaceful protests, violent riots, and increased attacks on law enforcement. A 2018 survey from the Pew Research Center revealed that 61 percent of people believe that police officers act unethically some or most of the time, and 45 percent do not think that police officers face serious consequences for unethical behavior (Varas, 2021).

Confidence in law enforcement officers is especially low among racial minorities. While 72 percent of White Americans believe that police officers treat racial and ethnic groups equally at least some time, only half of Hispanics and one-third of Black Americans believe the same. Similarly, a 2016 survey from the Cato Institute found that Black Americans (73 percent) and Hispanics (54 percent) are far more likely than Whites (35 percent) to believe that police are too quick to use lethal force. Black Americans are also twice as likely as White Americans to know someone physically abused by police and say those police tactics are generally too harsh (Varas, 2021).

These racial disparities in perception reflect fundamental differences in treatment given the same circumstances. As would be expected, if diminished faith in institutions leads people to withdraw from them, groups with low confidence in the police are less likely to cooperate with them. For example, Emily Ekins of the Cato Institute reports that Black Americans are much less likely than Whites to say they definitely would report a crime. Obviously, this is no recipe for improving community safety (Varas, 2021).

This mistrust in law enforcement on the part of Black and non-Black Americans has led to "defund the police" movements across the nation. Their proposals range from reforming police departments and focusing on community policing to calls for reducing police funding and allocating more dollars for social or job services. The most radical of these proposals call for the elimination of police departments altogether, leading to the demonization of police officers across the country (Varas, 2021).

America is facing a crisis of conscience. However, completely abolishing police would be an extreme response that would make our nation and communities less safe. First, exposure to violence is associated with a host of negative outcomes, including poor mental and physical health, problematic behaviors, poor academic performance and educational attainment, and even poor cognitive development. Police help to reduce violence and prevent these outcomes. According to academic research on police hiring grants in 2009, cities that experienced a 3.2 percent increase in police saw a 3.5 percent reduction in crime (Varas, 2021).

The movement toward community policing is also gaining momentum. Community policing is a different model of law enforcement based on trust. It has two components: community partnership and problem solving. Community policing requires police to develop positive relationships with the community, involve the community in crime control and prevention, and identify the community's specific concerns as well as the most appropriate remedies for them, which do not always involve the police (Varas, 2021).

Ultimately, the success of police reform will depend on the actions of communities. Citizens must—and do—recognize the contributions that police officers make, day-in and day-out, to keep the streets safe. But police officers have a duty to serve the communities they patrol and the residents of those communities whose tax dollars employ them. Even the most dedicated officers contribute to the erosion of community trust when they overlook wrongs committed by bad apples or support the efforts of unions to protect them. Removing barriers to police accountability would help prevent harmful police actions by officers who fail to live up to their duty, thus helping to increase trust in an institution largely made up of honorable men and women who serve to protect America's communities (Varas, 2021).

I never once resorted to *the "Us vs. Them"* **policing mindset to persecute or mistreat any citizen.** It is wrong to paint people with a broad brush because of their respective race, ethnicity, or community. Police officers must hold to their oath of office and do their job the right way. Unfortunately, this expectation remains an uphill battle for misguided police officers.

The *"Us vs. Them"* policing mindset is inexcusably provocative. It provokes unnecessary citizen complaints like racial profiling and the unreasonable use of excessive force. Rebellious officers with troublesome backgrounds are more likely to become victims burdened by costly lawsuits.

When not addressed appropriately by supervisors, patterns of unethical practices and policy violations lead to losing outcomes. Good police officers must safeguard against *"Bad Apples"* continually undermining public trust.

I chose to begin *"Misguided Badges"* with the Law Enforcement Code of Ethics. I will end it focused on the same. The Code of Ethics is a universal standard that governs commitment, respect, and integrity. It is imperative that police officers clearly understand their moral obligations of trust and accountability in our democratic society.

As peace officers or guardians – not warriors – police officers shall uphold their Oath of Office with the highest standards of ethical conduct. The definition of a *'warrior'* is a *soldier or fighter,'* which implies violence. On the other hand, the purpose of *'guardian'* is a *'defender, protector, or keeper'* who advocates for another. This approach – ultimately a change in mindset – can help build trust between officers and civilians and prevent unnecessary use of force (Gasior, 2017).

American policing must hold to the fundamental principles and values it represents, free from the racism, brutality, and hypocrisy that tarnishes it. Accordingly, police officers who ascribe to bias, bigotry, ignorance, and hate must change for the sake of surviving in 21st Century law enforcement. More leadership and commitment are yet expected of Police officials to change discriminatory policies and reevaluate practices across the country.

I appreciate your reading and understanding my purpose for speaking out with honesty and conviction. I remain prayerful and optimistic for our American policing culture. I challenge others to do the same. Police officers are necessary for public safety in a free and diverse society. As a Black boy, I grew up confused and living a lie about police officers. Regardless, I wish not to die with the lie believing that all police officers are good guys.

Law enforcement officers must safeguard the public's trust to perform their jobs effectively. Because ethical conduct significantly impacts public trust, law enforcement agencies must closely examine their policies, reward systems, and training to ensure that their agency fosters a culture of firm ethical values.

Instead of expecting that officers already possess a firmly engrained set of values (good or bad) when they enter the police force, managers must remember that all officers have the potential to act virtuously; but, when the work environment allows misbehavior either implicitly or explicitly, the potential for abuse skyrockets. Theognis of Megara, another ancient Greek philosopher, said, *"Fairly examined, truly understood, no man is wholly bad, nor wholly good."* Police officers are not exempt from this idea. Influential law enforcement leaders bring out the best in their staff by ensuring that officers not only understand the right thing to do but do it (Fitch, 2011).

MISGUIDED BADGES, *a Memoir,* is my message of TRUTH to remind police officers, court prosecutors, and partisan politicians of their oath of office and moral obligation to pursue equal justice -- under the rule of law -- for all American citizens.

I encourage *Misguided Police Officers* to pick up their broken pieces of BIAS, BIGOTRY, and HATRED for the sake of American democracy. Remember, America is recognized globally as one nation, under GOD, that prides itself on free-thinking, inalienable rights, and equal justice. Let us remain prayerful despite the abusive practices and bizarre ignorance that divide misguided police officers and Black citizens. Keep the faith; GOD ALMIGHTY is still in control.

Captain D. Terry Yarbrough

About The Author

D. Terry Yarbrough, a native Memphian, aka Denver T. Yarbrough, started his law enforcement career, March 4, 1968, with the Memphis Police Department (MPD), in Memphis, Tennessee. January 9, 1984, Yarbrough resigned from MPD, in good standing, with 16 years of service. August 12, 1985, Yarbrough joined the Shelby County Sheriff's Office (SCSO). August 31, 2013, he retired from SCSO with 28 years of service earning the rank of Captain.

Captain Yarbrough was later appointed the Chief of Police of Mason, Tennessee, from September 12, 2016, to February 21, 2019. After that, Yarbrough marketed his professional services as a law enforcement consultant.

Yarbrough is a graduate of Memphis Hamilton High School. He later earned a Bachelor of Arts Degree in Criminal Justice, cum laude, from LeMoyne-Owen College, in Memphis, Tennessee. He is a December 1996 graduate of the FBI National Academy (FBINA), Session 187, at Quantico, Virginia. Completing the FBI National Academy law enforcement program was a tremendous asset to his professional career.

Yarbrough, a lifetime member of the National Organization of Black Law Enforcement Executives (NOBLE), is a past president of the NOBLE West Tennessee Chapter. Also, Yarbrough treasures his membership with the International Association of Chiefs of Police (IACP); FBI

National Academy Associates (FBINAA) Tennessee Chapter; Fraternal Order of Police (FOP) Shelby Metro Lodge 35; Tennessee Sheriff's Association (TSA); and National Sheriff's Association (NSA). In 2014, Yarbrough volunteered to serve on the Memphis-Shelby County Juvenile Court Foster Care Review Board. He continues to maintain a passionate interest in youth mentoring, cultural enrichment, and athletic development programs.

Yarbrough embraces a community policing philosophy focused on what counts "the People," regardless of race, gender, ethnicity, address, economic status, political preference, or religious practice. He believes that building trust is an asset to establishing relationships, promoting best practices, and deterring lawlessness. He remains committed to quality training and the highest standards of ethical conduct. Yarbrough's career combined 46 years of service at three Tennessee agencies.

"Remember, It's Never the Wrong Time
to Do the Right Thing!"
-- *DTY*

Misguided Badges

References

Associated Press. (2019, June 6). Five States Investigate Racist, Violent Posts by Police. Retrieved from https://www.courthousenews.com/five-states-investigate-racist-violent-posts-by-police/

Berkow, I. (1996, September 17) *Joe Elsby Martin, 80, Muhammad Ali's First Boxing Teacher.* Retrieved from Joe Elsby Martin, 80, Muhammad Ali's First Boxing Teacher - The New York Times (nytimes.com)

Bradley, C. (2019, February 28) *Beyond the Memphis State Eight: The civil rights fight for equality at the University of Memphis.* Retrieved from https://www.highgroundnews.com/features/MemphisStateCivilRights.aspx

Brown, D.L., (2018, February 12) *I Am a Man: The ugly Memphis sanitation workers' strike that led to MLK's assassination.* Retrieved from https://www.washingtonpost.com/news/retropolis/wp/2018/02/12/i-am-a-man-the-1968-memphis-sanitation-workers-strike-that-led-to-mlks-assassination/

Capriel, J. (2014, June 21) *As one of the first black Memphis officers in 1949, Williams helped blaze a trail.* Retrieved from https://insurancenewsnet.com/oarticle/As-one-of-first-black-Memphis-officers-in-1949-Williams-helped-blaze-a-trail-a-520734#.XxG4B55KjIU

Charles Koch Institute. (n.d.). *Role of Police in America.* https://www.charleskochinstitute.org/issue-areas/criminal-justice-policing-reform/role-of-police-in-america/

Corbould, C. (2020, June 2) *The fury in U.S. cities is rooted in a long history of racist policing, violence, and equality.* Retrieved from https://theconversation.com/the-fury-in-us-cities-is-rooted-in-a-long-history-of-racist-policing-violence-and-inequality-139752 (Updated June 2, 2020, 9:26 am AEST)

Conover, T. (2018, January/February) *Smithsonian Magazine: The Strike That Brought MLK to Memphis.* Retrieved from http://tedconover.com/2018/01/the-strike-that-brought-mlk-to-memphis/

Darnell, D. (1973, December 7) *NOT GUILTY.* Retrieved from Not Guilty - 175 Moments | The Commercial Appeal

D'Auria, P. (2021, June 17) *The Jersey Journal: Hudson Catholic High School pulls assignment comparing police killings to lynchings.* Retrieved from https://www.nj.com/hudson/2021/06/hudson-catholic-high-school-pulls-assignment-comparing-police-killings-to-lynchings.html

Davis, A.J., Henning, K. (2017, May 25) *Opinion: How policing Black boys leads to the conditioning of Black men.* Retrieved from https://www.bleausa.org/opinion-how-policing-black-boys-leads-to-the-conditioning-of-black-men/

Edwards, C. (2016, February 16) *Race and the Police.* Retrieved from https://www.policefoundation.org/race-and-the-police/

Fitch, B.D., (2011, October 1) *Rethinking Ethics in Law Enforcement.* Retrieved from https://leb.fbi.gov/articles/focus/focus-on-ethics-rethinking-ethics-in-law-enforcement

Goggans, L. (2014, June 26) *True Blue – Memphis Lawmen of 1948 looks at the first nine Black MPD officers.* Retrieved from https://m.memphisflyer.com/memphis/documentary-highlights-mpds-1948-integration/Content?oid=3692945

Gramlich, J. (2017, January 12) *Black and white officers see many key aspects of policing differently.* Retrieved from https://www.pewresearch.org/fact-tank/2017/01/12/black-and-white-officers-see-many-key-aspects-of-policing-differently/?amp=1

Gasior, M., (2017, July 4) *Adopting the Guardian Mindset.* Retrieved from https://www.powerdms.com/blog/adopting-the-guardian-mindset/

Hannah-Jones, N. (2015, March 4) *Yes, Black America Fears the Police. Here's Why.* Retrieved from Yes, Black America Fears the Police. Here's Why. — ProPublica

Hansen, C. (2019, July 10) *Slave Patrols: An Early Form of American Policing.* Retrieved from https://lawenforcementmuseum.org/2019/07/10/slave-patrols-an-early-form-of-american-policing/

Harriot, M. (2019, June 15) *Report: Hundreds of police officers belong to racist Facebook groups.* Retrieved from https://www.theroot.com/report-hundreds-of-police-officers-belong-to-racist-fa-1835542308/amp

Hinton, R. (2021, April 19) *Lawmaker wants police officers taught how racism, 'ignorance' prevent them from doing their job fairly.* Retrieved from https://chicago.suntimes.com/2021/4/19/22392451/critical-race-theory-police-officers-racism-race-lashawn-ford-fop-catanzara

Honey, M. (2018, February 9) *MLK's '68 struggle for economic justice still marching on.* Retrieved from https://www.commercialappeal.com/story/opinion/contributors/2018/02/09/mlks-68-struggle-economic-justice-still-marching/323872002/

Hudson, R. (2016, July 7) *I'm a black ex-cop, and this is the real truth about race and policing.* Retrieved from https://www.vox.com/platform/amp/2015/5/28/8661977/race-police-officer

Ingram, H. (2020, June 25) *'Wipe them off the map': Three Wilmington police officers fired for racist comments.* Retrieved from https://www.courier-tribune.com/news/20200625/lsquowipe-them-off-maprsquo-three-wilmington-police-officers-fired-for-racist-comments?template=ampart

Jean-Phillips, M., Williams, E. (2018, April 16) *Why DC Police Are Studying Critical Race Theory.* Retrieved from https://www.washingtonian.com/2018/04/16/dc-police-critical-race-theory-nmaahc-bernie-demczuk-sharita-thompson/

Jones, R.F. (2021, August 19) *Black Boxers and Golden Gloves, from Segregation to National Champions.* Retrieved from Black Boxers and Golden Gloves, from Segregation to National Champions · Notable Kentucky African Americans Database (uky.edu)

Kaplan, J., Sapien, J. (2021, January 14) *No One Took Us Seriously: Black Cops Warned About Racist Capitol Police Officers for Years.* Retrieved from https://www.propublica.org/article/no-one-took-us-seriously-black-cops-warned-about-racist-capitol-police-officers-for-years

Miles, T. (2016 September 23) *U.S. police killings reminiscent of lynching, U.N. group says.* Retrieved from https://news.yahoo.com/u-police-killings-reminiscent-lynching-u-n-group-142912740.html

Miller, J., Ray, R. (2019, November 4) *Highlights: Improving police culture in America.* Retrieved from: https://www.brookings.edu/blog/up-front/2019/11/04/highlights-improving-police-culture-in-america/

Mordock, J. (2020, June 28) *Morale is lower with the White officers in the wake of George Floyd's death in police custody.* Retrieved from https://m.washingtontimes.com/news/2020/jun/28/black-cops-say-systemic-racism-exists-policing/

National Public Radio. (2020, June 18) *What It Is Like to Be a Black Police Officer.* Retrieved from: https://www.npr.org/2020/06/18/880513767/what-it-is-like-to-be-a-black-police-officer

Neuman, S. (2020, July 9) *Police Viewed Less Favorably, But Few Want To 'Defund' Them, Survey Finds.*
Retrieved from https://www.npr.org/sections/live-updates-protests-for-racial-justice/2020/07/09/889618702/police-viewed-less-favorably-but-few-want-to-defund-them-survey-finds

Odell, R. (2020, May 11) *Beale Street, and the 1968 Sanitation Worker's Strike.* Retrieved from: https://owlcation.com/humanities/What-Happened-In-Memphis-After-Kings-Death-In-1968

Richards, E., Wong, A. (2021, September 10) *Parents want kids to learn about ongoing effects of slavery – but not critical race theory. They're the same thing.* Retrieved from Parents want kids to learn about ongoing effects of slavery – but not critical race theory. They're the same thing. (newscon.net)

Robertson, G.L. (2021, September 2) *Bipartisan North Carolina police reform signed by Cooper.* Retrieved from Bipartisan North Carolina police reforms signed by Cooper (apnews.com)

Rodriguez, I. (2021, March 2) *Stop Turning Your Head: Black Cops Speak Out Against Blanket of Racism.* Retrieved from Stop Turning Your Head: Black Cops Speak Out Against 'Blanket of Racism' | The Crime Report

Rosen, J. (2017, February 2) *The Black Patrolmen of 1940s Memphis.* Retrieved from https://www.mentalfloss.com/article/66775/black-patrolmen-1940s-memphis

Rosenbloom, J. (2018, March 25) *How Memphis police leaders failed Martin Luther King Jr.* Retrieved from: https://www.salon.com/2018/03/25/how-memphis-police-leaders-failed-martin-luther-king-jr/

Savannah Tribune. (2021, June 30) *Critical Race Theory-What Is All the Fuss About?* Retrieved from: https://www.savannahtribune.com/articles/critical-race-theory-what-is-all-the-fuss-about/

Sullivan, T. (2020, June 1) *OPINION: Louisville can still learn from the lessons a cop taught Muhammad Ali.* Retrieved from https://www.courier-journal.com/story/sports/2020/06/01/police-athletic-league-ceo-sees-a-part-for-us-to-play-as-louisville-considers-its-own-chapter/5308312002/

The Crime Report. (2008, n.d.) *Our Mission / The Crime Report.* Retrieved from Our Mission | The Crime Report

Turner, K.B., Giacopassi, D., & Vandiver, M. (2006). Ignoring the Past: Coverage of Slavery and Slave Patrols in Criminal Justice Texts. Journal of Criminal Justice Education, 17: (1), 181-195.
Tri-State Defender. (1964, February 15). Shug Jones to retire. *The Tri-State Defender*, pp. A1, A2. https://digitalcommons.murraystate.edu/tsd/7

Varas, J. (2021, March 22) *Accountability for Bad Apples: Police Reforms to Restore Faith in Institutions.* Retrieved from Accountability for Bad Apples: Police Reforms to Restore Faith in Institutions - Accountability for Bad Apples: Police Reforms to Restore Faith in Institutions - United States Joint Economic Committee (senate.gov)

Vecsey, G. (1971, December 10) *9 Lawmen Charged in Death of Black Memphis Youth.* 9 Lawmen Charged in Death of Black Memphis Youth - The New York Times (nytimes.com)

Vecsey, G. (1971, October 23) *2 Memphis Boys Hopeful on Inquiry.* Retrieved from 2 Memphis Boys Hopeful on Inquiry - The New York Times (nytimes.com)

Volpe, M. (2020, November 17) *The Roots and Reach of Critical Race Theory.* Retrieved from: https://www.theamericanconservative.com/articles/the-roots-and-reach-of-critical-race-theory/

Captain D. Terry Yarbrough

Misguided Badges

Made in the USA
Coppell, TX
20 February 2022

73857915R00092